rhetoric of
BLACK
REVOLUTION

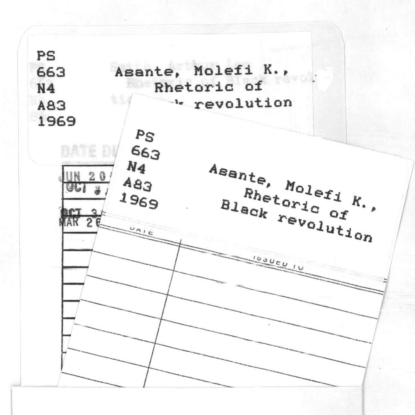

rhetoric of
BLACK
REVOLUTION

ARTHUR L. SMITH

University of California
at Los Angeles

Allyn and Bacon, Inc., Boston

FOR JEAN

Second printing . . . July, 1970

Contents

v

Preface

No period in American history has been so thoroughly volatile with the rhetoric of militant blacks as the last fifteen years. With the emergence of Martin Luther King, Jr., as the great moral force in the struggle for equality, Americans looked forward to the idyllic state when prejudice and racism would give way to the dreamed of brotherhood. But King was killed. Even before the murder of the eloquent drum major for justice, the civil rights movement appeared to be exhausting itself. The decline of the nonviolent campaign was accompanied by the rising voices of Black Power advocates and black nationalists who insisted on human rights for all Americans at any cost whatsoever. Where King and others had pleaded, the militants demanded. In city after city, enraged blacks went on rampage against what they considered the system of their oppression.

This book is an attempt to discuss the origins, context, strategies, topics, and audience of the rhetoric of black revolution. The term black revolution is used in the broad sense of drastic, immediate change in the social, political, or economic structure.

In the first chapter, I have sought to describe in limited detail the rhetorical situation that produces and sustains the rhetoric of black revolution. This chapter necessarily deals with the nature of the rhetoric insofar as that rhetoric is

aggressive and unifying. In a second chapter, I have indicated the kinds of rhetorical designs employed by the
militant black spokesmen, pointing out examples of the use
of these designs. Then in a third chapter I have given attention to the prevailing themes in the rhetoric of black
revolution, suggesting that there is a difference between the
topics espoused by the religious rhetors and those proclaimed by the secular rhetors. In a short fourth chapter, I
have sketched in uncertain outline the nature of the black
audience. Seeking the sources of contemporary black
rhetoric in a fifth chapter, I have studied the rhetorical
origins of the black revolution. This chapter sought to
identify the legacies of David Walker, Charles Remond,
Frederick Douglass, Marcus Garvey, and W. E. B. Du Bois
for the present rhetors of black revolution. Finally, I have
ended with a sixth chapter of selected speeches from black
rhetors.

The broad scope of this topic will, I hope, make this
book a valuable asset to teachers and students of English,
sociology, and American history.

To the extent that this book will help to clarify the
rhetoric expressed by the militant blacks, it is hoped that it
will contribute to more effective communication between
blacks and whites. For it is impossible to communicate with
a man if you do not know what he is saying or why he is
saying it. I submit this work, then, seeking to add to the
appreciation of the necessity of effective human communication.

Arthur L. Smith

1

Toward a Revolutionary Rhetoric

Every revolution has rhetoric that attempts to justify the claims and legitimize the aspirations of the revolutionists; the black revolution is no exception. During the American Revolution, for example, the dissident voices of Samuel Adams, James Otis, and Patrick Henry verbalized the sentiments and moods of a people suffering the violence of oppression. In much the same way, the contemporary black social revolution possesses a unique rhetoric that speaks to and for the black masses.

The terms employed must signify unity and aggressiveness for the revolutionists' rhetoric. A revolutionary rhetoric must possess an offensive stance if it is to mold the beliefs of the masses into a tight compact against the *status quo* opinion. Thus, all revolutionary rhetoric is essentially aggressive rather than defensive. The aggression inherent in revolutionary rhetoric becomes a unifying force that gives revolutionists a mien of tremendous energy.

Rhetoric of revolution, then, is distinguished by a fluidity that depends on the linguistic components of the language as much as the grievances of the revolutionists. Indeed, the one is partly dependent on the other. Without grievance, distress, and political or social discomfort, a revolution lacks the necessary fuel on which to base its power. Thus, all effective revolutions have been for equality, justice, and dignity.

1

In an article in the *William and Mary Quarterly*, Gordon S. Wood expresses a belief that revolutions must be based on genuine grievances.[1] But what people believe their situation to be is a crucial factor in their susceptibility to revolutionary rhetoric. As long as the revolutionists believe that grievances exist, for rhetorical purposes they do exist. As Wood indicates, the American colonists were probably not the most persecuted people of their time, either economically, politically, or socially.[2] Yet the American colonists had a violent revolution. It was a revolution, then, created in part by the articulation of grievances in a dynamic linguistic aggression that tended to exaggerate the colonists' complaints.

Despite its fluidity, revolutionary rhetoric has some features of any other rhetoric. Rhetoric is concerned with the communication of ideas, values, opinions, and beliefs in an effort to elicit the approval or acceptance of others. Within his particular situation, the rhetor attempts to discover means with which to show the aptness of his message. Insofar as the revolutionist seeks to find the means of persuasion within a given rhetorical situation, he functions as a rhetor.

The present rhetoric of black revolution first appeared after the Montgomery bus boycott and the Supreme Court School Decision of 1954, *Brown vs. Board of Education*. Before these events, the policies of the NAACP and the eloquence of Martin Luther King, Jr., had directed and inspired the Black masses. After these events, black nationalists, black Muslims, and their sympathizers increasingly preached revolution as the panacea of the black predicament. Their rhetoric, essentially different from that of King and the Montgomery Improvement Association, is reminiscent of David Walker, W. E. B. Du Bois and to a lesser extent, Marcus Garvey.[3]

[1] Gordon S. Wood, "Rhetoric and Reality in the American Revolution," William and Mary Quarterly, XXIII, ser. 3, (1966), p. 4.
[2] *Ibid.*
[3] David Walker, author of the 1829 pamphlet AN APPEAL TO THE

The early rhetoric of black revolution was characterized by aggression against whites, who were portrayed as the conveyers of racist attitudes and values. Simultaneously, this rhetoric tried to create black unity. Externally, the outlook was aggressive; internally, the search was for unity. Little attempt was made to appeal to white America in the traditional rhetorical context. The black revolutionists did not seek the approval or acceptance of their ideas by their white audiences. Contrarily, they seemed to seek rejection by the white audience. White rejection, however, usually guaranteed black unity, and this was precisely the revolutionist's aim. For example, some black revolutionists asked that blacks be left alone to set up their own state, to seek their own economic development, and to assert their manhood. It should not be suggested that it was a rhetoric pleading for acceptance, for the black revolutionists were calling for the effective separation and even alienation of the two races.

The message of these black revolutionists is both frightening and hopeful. The terrifying fact is the futility of the rhetorical aim of those seeking a separate land for blacks. In one speech, Malcolm X voiced the sentiment, "We want our own land right here in America."[4] But what is contained in that sentence is an impossibility inherent in America. To grant blacks a separate state or states in America would be to destroy America. Even though it may be possible to understand the despair, alienation, and anxiety that bring on the land demands by black revolutionists, their rhetoric fails insofar as it seeks intrinsically impossible demands of the nation. Yet the rhetors' indictment of white America is that it could not and would not relinquish any

COLOURED CITIZENS OF THE WORLD, was the first militant black to have a significant impact on white America. W. E. B. Du Bois challenged Booker T. Washington's social philosophy by insisting on full social, economic, and political equality for blacks. Marcus Garvey led the largest mass movement of Afro-Americans during the 1920's. His rhetoric emphasized black dignity, self-respect, and a return to Africa.

[4]Malcolm X, "Message to the Grass Roots," long playing record published by the Afro-American Broadcasting and Recording Company, Detroit, 1965. (The speech was given to the Northern Negro Grass Roots Leadership Conference, Detroit, November 20, 1963.)

land without a loss of national purpose. Part of the American mythology involves the impossibility of the separate states assertion. What is intricately included in this impossibility is the notion of a national destiny, or dream, or goal of a new and more equitable world order. To allow separate states for blacks within the boundary of the United States would nullify united in the national term and destroy the nation's social and political mythology. Since no rhetoric can be successful unless it is consistent with or effectively overcomes the listener's mythology, this aspect of the black nationalists' rhetoric is profoundly unconvincing to most Americans.

The conjecture can be made that the black nationalists who made land demands anticipated rejection, despite their vehement agitation. Indeed, it seems unlikely that the rhetors expected the American nation to grant their radical demands, if only because of the verbal commitment to fraternity among the American peoples by the recent Federal administrations. But the black nationalists also knew that with their rhetoric they had placed the spotlight on a basic American dilemma, exposing a festering sore in the nation's body politic.

A dilemma that the black nationalists verbalize for white Americans is: How can we divorce ourselves from the blacks and at the same time maintain our national integrity? The nationalists have consistently argued that America does not want the blacks integrated in the nation. During the 1968 national elections, black nationalists were heard saying, "Most whites want to vote for Wallace; even if they don't, they want to."[5] But the difficulty of the dilemma as stated can be appreciated when it is realized that many blacks consider themselves American and believe the national mythology as firmly as do other persons. More significant than expected rejection is the fact that the black nationalists posed the question in the first place. This indicates that they were aware of the impending impasse for

[5]Speech given by Walter Bremond at University of Southern California, Los Angeles, August, 1968.

white Americans. The aggressiveness of their rhetoric was demonstrated: once they perceived the essential contradiction in American society, they heightened the dilemma by voicing their separate states suggestion. Whatever else may have been their intentions, the black nationalists succeeded in showing that whites were not willing to go forward (in their terms) one way or the other. Of course, the black nationalists were attempting to prove that if anything could be said concerning white America, it was that there existed unanimity only on one issue: the social *status quo*.

Because their rhetoric contains both the language of aggression and unification, the black nationalists have issued a specialized call for community. No effort is made to unify America; all energy is expended for inducing unity among black Americans. The black nationalists contend that the unity of black Americans is a necessary step for the eventual unity of the nation.[6] Thus, such phrases as black is beautiful, let's get ourselves together, and most important Black Power have become common in the black community as rallying expressions for unity.

Meant for black people as a unifying rhetoric, these phrases and slogans like them seem to have been taken by the press and other media as particularly terrifying. Perhaps, terrifying because they are aggressive terms that contradict white America's view of the docile Negro. But if these phrases produce a certain dissonance for white Americans, for blacks they signal the dawn of a new era. In the words of one black nationalist, "They are black words and phrases defined by blacks for blacks."[7] In 1967 in Los Angeles, Stokely Carmichael was pressed by two white reporters for his definition of Black Power. Carmichael insisted that he would not define the terms, that they had meaning for black people, and that if white people did not understand them, then that was their hang-up.[8] Obviously if these

[6]Malcolm X, *Malcolm X Speaks,* edited by George Breitman, New York: Merit, p. 21.
[7]Interview given by Stokely Carmichael, Los Angeles, May 1967. (The author was present during this interview.)
[8]*Ibid.*

words are understood by blacks and suspected as something devious or sinister by whites, the nationalists have again become aggressors and unifiers. Black nationalists insist that white Americans are terrified when "black" is combined with "power." When Black Power is mentioned, whites tend to conjure up scenes of violence, which causes the black nationalists to ask, what has White Power meant? A black student at a California state college complained recently that the white advisor of their black student organization had confided to him that he would feel more comfortable with the "Negro Club" than with the Black Students Action Group. For blacks, the word "Negro" is hopelessly stereotyped; but for whites, it is comfortable. With this rhetoric of definition and redefinition, the black nationalists have succeeded in getting most whites off balance in their effort to force white Americans to see this nation's social predicament.

In the practice of this rhetoric, keeping the opponent off balance becomes a key strategy. Like the other rhetors of the black revolution, the black nationalists attack; they seldom defend. A good offensive rhetoric is considered a good measure of defense because the opposition must use his energy to refute the charges pressed against him.

For example, the black rhetor says, "The whites are hated all around the world," or "LBJ is a buffoon," or "America is a racist country."[9] These charges keep the opposition in motion to deny, to defend, to support, and to safeguard, while the black revolutionist is free to launch new attacks in different socio-political areas. The rhetorical strategy is based on this rationale of movement: Anything that facilitates black unity is good; anything that indicts white America is good.

These rhetorical moves are apparently calculated to terrify the whites and to unify the blacks. On the one hand, they are terrifying because of their mystery, indefiniteness, and even, vagueness; on the other, unifying because they

---

[9]See Charles Lomas, *The Agitator in American Society*, Englewood: Prentice-Hall, 1968, pp. 135–151.

give blacks their own power words and terms. One black rhetor remarked after President Johnson's civil rights speech in which he said, "We shall overcome," that the president "wouldn't dare get on TV and say, 'We want Black Power.' "[10] The effect of these terms and phrases seems to be to give coherence to a confused despair and to canalize the sentiments and emotions of black people toward an object outside themselves.

The fluidity of this rhetoric is sensed when the revolutionists insist on redefining their situational culture in a way that liberates them while it imprisons the whites. Specifically, the black revolutionists are concerned with identity, black identity in a white world. Their rhetoric also becomes a rhetoric of redefinition as they grapple with terms like *Negritude*, Negro, Afro-Americans, black, natural, and brother. In the identity crisis, each revolutionist has to hew out his own definition from the forest of cultural possibilities in an effort to elicit response from his audience when he appeals to them on the basis of this new definition. For example, Maulana Karenga's "Negro" may not come off as menacingly as H. Rap Brown's, and yet the term is repugnant to each of them. Redefinition means a reshaping of the black man's universe to upgrade black people.

Of course, the question of the white man's place will have to be answered before the black universe can achieve stability. But the rhetoric of most black revolutionists attempts to avoid that question. "We have no time to be concerned with the white man's problems," the black revolutionist is often heard to say.[11] The Black Muslims have tried to answer the question of the white man in a black universe by defining the white man as a "devil" created by an evil black scientist. Their metaphysics have failed to impress many blacks who must deal with the "devil" every day.

[10]Speech given by Maulana Karenga at Purdue University, December 9, 1968.
[11]Speech given by Minister Franklin Florence at Purdue University, October, 1968.

What redefinition means to the black revolutionists is that the whites will have to bargain on black terms and understand the world as constructed by blacks. Thus, whites are often entangled in a quandary of definition: black power, soul brother, and *Negritude*.

To the unsophisticated white audiences, these terms suggest a unique separateness on the part of the black man, maybe even prejudice. Other whites view these terms, whether defined or not, as a search for identity and relationship. And yet the imprisonment of the whites is accomplished in either case, for now they are doing the viewing, rather than the defining. Some whites are uncomfortable because the definitions are no longer being provided by their stereotype of the "Negro." Furthermore, the basis is established for a better rhetoric because it is the first time that a significant number of blacks have addressed themselves so engagingly to their total liberation. Proposing new vocabularies, seeking white attitudinal reform, and calling for a restructuring of our national concerns, the black revolutionists have questioned the essence of the American experience. And for a rhetoric to be relevant, it must go beyond the superficial and strike at reality. Perhaps this explains the reluctance of the nation to accept or believe the revolutionists. No one can continue to accept the American experience without first reckoning with the rhetoric of the black rhetors. To suggest that this is an egalitarian country or that all people share in the American promise is an absurdity in the light of the overwhelming data, experienced and cited by the votarists of the black movement. Clearly this is a new era in the American socio-political experience because large numbers of blacks have begun to speak to the essential American paradoxes for which white America has few resolutions.

The situation in which whites held the key even to the black man's definition of himself no longer exists. As one black revolutionist puts it, "Those cats gave us Negro, black in Spanish; but since we speak English, baby, we're going to be black in English. They can't get 'nigger' from that like they could from 'Negro.' Now they will have to be satisfied with our blackness."[12] Blacks seem to believe that there is some truth in the old adage, "the namer of names is always the father of things." To be defined by whites is to remain a slave, and slavery is anything but a pleasant memory to the black race. Thus his rhetoric shows new assertiveness, movement, aggressiveness, as he refuses to allow the white man to define his identity.

Since the black revolutionists see the search for black identity as depending on complete acceptance of blackness, they tell their audiences to get African names for their children, to wear *dashikis*, to wear the *au naturel* haircuts, and to help themselves by refusing to accept white hand-outs.

The re-emergence of black nations in Africa has considerably influenced the rhetoric of the black revolution. African travel rather than European travel is urged on the black masses. For example, a few years ago, a glance through *Jet* magazine would have revealed very few blacks traveling to Africa; but there was seldom an issue that did not have a story of a black person touring the European capitals. The rhetoric of the black revolutionists has seemingly influenced a rediscovery of the black Americans' African heritage. Evidence of this is also seen in the popularity of Afro-American as a name for black Americans. This term takes into account both African heritage and American nationality.

Essentially, the black revolutionists' aim is to preach pride, self-respect, and self-assertion. Because of this stance, bleaching creams, processed hair, and even the conventional Western hair comb have become despicable symbols of black slavery to white values. While I was doing research for this book, a young black lady said to me, "The white people made the forks in the combs close together for their hair, not for ours." The revolutionist assumes that bleaching creams and processed hair destroy the power of any black self-assertion because the black man becomes a seeker of white values. Karenga (who changed his name from Ron

[12]*Ibid.*

Everett) decries the black man who goes to an integrated party and tries to speak like the whites. To Karenga, this is a clear case of 'copping out.' Nor does he take kindly to the black man who refuses to see the value of wearing African dress. Thus, Karenga's organization US has started making Afro-American outfits to be sold in black communities. Pride and self-respect are the twin concepts that keep the rhetoric in motion in the black communities.

Even the churches have been affected by the secularistic emphasis on racial pride, where heretofore the churches concentrated on preaching the deliverance of God. Black values are enhanced by the rhetoric, and a sense of coherence is presented for the black community.

By asking the black community to find its salvation within itself, the black revolutionist gives a sense of independence that was never produced, nor could ever be produced by white rhetoric regardless of how liberal that rhetoric appeared to be. Its support, however earnest and honest, carried with it the sting of paternalism. Whether the rhetoric was uttered by a president or a mayor made little difference to the black revolutionists, except as it may have been a method for restraining white racism. Even though it was clear that blacks could not make social progress without the relaxation of white discrimination, the black revolutionists also understood that the black masses had to 'get themselves together.' The possibility of black success resides largely with the white community. But even without massive support from the white community, the rhetoric of the black revolutionists makes powerful medicine and might lead to recovery of black pride.

Even more dramatic and significant than black unity is the black revolutionists' insistence that the black people are the only salvation of the nation. Black rhetors see in the intrigues of international politics the need for a rending of the fabric of America. Haranguing crowds of depressed and oppressed people, the rhetors proclaim the doom of America if the black people fail to save the nation. Furthermore, the world will only escape destruction by the efforts of the colored peoples (as opposed to the colorless peoples) because the whites are too degenerate.

The rhetors insist that redefinition plays a significant role in the nation's salvation. Karenga, particularly, is fond of saying that when the whites define the peoples of the world, they put all other peoples on the defensive. To say 'nonwhite' is abominable to the rhetors of black revolution because to accept nonwhite is to be defined by whites. On the other hand, Karenga argues that the colored peoples of the world, including Mexican-Americans, Japanese, and Malayans, must refuse to be defined by the white man.[13] Some black rhetors have asked their audiences, "What would the white man think if we started referring to him as nonblack?" While this appears to be a game, it is nonetheless a serious attempt by the black man to transcend the slavery experience.

It is this optimism within the present upsurge in black identity that validates the rhetoric that seeks to destroy and construct. Throughout the anxious speeches and activities of the black revolutionists, this tension is brought on by a mission to tear down and at the same time to build. To whites, Stokely Carmichael and H. Rap Brown appeared to be spokesmen of destruction. But to most black audiences, their message is one of restoration that has been needed so long and so desperately. Even though their rhetoric is seldom associated with violence, it does suggest the need to destroy racist institutions; this is the threat of violence.

Until the black revolutionists began pronouncing their prescriptions for what they called a sick society, most Americans were content with the token accomplishments of social legislation. When the black revolutionists came with a different rhetoric from that of Martin Luther King, Jr., Bayard Rustin, and Roy Wilkins, their voices were like prophets of doom from the wilderness. In a nation where King, Rustin, and Wilkins were considered radicals, the black revolutionists, who called for a more authentic revolution, were

[13]Speech given by Maulana Karenga to the United Mexican American Students at University of California, Los Angeles, May, 1968.

anathema. Whereas Martin Luther King, Jr., had been content with the gradual change brought about through protest and social legislation, the black revolutionists saw the immediate deliverance of the black masses in political leverage, economic control of the ghettoes, and self-assertion. They argued that the black man could never be free until he accepted and asserted his freedom even in the face of physical death.

The black revolutionists introduced a new dynamism identified by pride and self-respect into the black community. Now blacks were speaking of "our brothers in Africa" when only a few years before they would have scorned the suggestion. The black masses had been galvanized by the strange message of black identity, and as Karenga has said, this was their ultimate reality.[14] No longer seeking to receive, they wanted to be able to give. Tired of begging, they intended to earn or take, as circumstances dictated.

Involved in the black man's new awareness was an acceptance of things black, an acceptance of the Dark Continent, the epitome of blackness. Given the American situation with political juggling of social legislation, disdain for the black man's cry of police brutality, the South's lack of will to enforce the 1954 Supreme Court School Desegregation Decision, *Brown vs. Board of Education*, white backlash, and many other injustices, the black revolutionists decided that the white man had no intention to move until the black man did. Thus, only in this grasping for black awareness could the black masses really come to grips with themselves and their American predicament.

The message of the revolutionists to the masses was that they had to re-trod their dismal past until they arrived, beyond slavery and exploitation, to the land where black men were born free. In seeing this, the black revolutionists were more advanced in their concept of social action than was Martin Luther King, Jr., because they knew that America

[14]Maulana Karenga, *The Quotable Karenga*, edited by Clyde Halisi and James MTume, Los Angeles: US Organization, 1967, p. 3.

was not yet able to provide them with a rationale for identity sufficient for liberation. Bombarded by Shakespeare, Milton, Emerson, and Poe, the blacks now believed that they also needed Phyllis Wheatley, Paul Laurence Dunbar, and Countee Cullen, Americans of African descent.[15] Confronted with European cultures that had never really accepted the black man, the revolutionists now saw the need for emphasis on African cultures. Had the American people respected the African's heritage, schools would have taught courses dealing with African cultures as well as with European cultures. But American education has all but ignored the existence of the black man, except during slavery. To make up for this omission, the black revolutionists have sought to re-indoctrinate the black masses with their history. Thus, acceptance of kinky hair, broad nose, and black skin, coupled with a knowledge of black history, in short, an identification and association with Africa and blackness, have produced a new consciousness of black manhood.

More than an accusation against the American society, this rhetoric of manhood initiated by the black revolutionists was an indictment of white liberal rhetoric in America. The rhetoric of white America was bound to fail because it could not appropriate satisfaction for white Anglo-Saxon Protestants and also for blacks up from slavery.

Inasmuch as rhetoric must have an audience because communication is a reciprocal process, the black revolutionists needed receivers for their message. To an extent, they inherited a ready-made audience. The audience of Martin Luther King, Jr., was especially susceptible to the rhetoric of the black revolutionists. He had prepared them intellectually and emotionally for acceptance of their dignity and manhood by demonstrating that they could get results by unity. Taking their cue from this point, the black revolutionists

[15]In 1773, Phyllis Wheatley, a Boston slave, published the first volume of verse by an Afro-American. Paul Laurence Dunbar was the first black poet to be recognized as a major creative artist. He published hundreds of poems in dialect and literary English. Countee Cullen was a leader of the Black Renaissance that swept Harlem during the 1920's and '30's.

declared that freedom had always come when men asserted themselves. Understandably it was not a great distance between "We shall overcome" and "We want Black Power." In saying that Dr. King's audience was prepared for the black revolutionists, I am not contending that the revolutionists did not have audiences of their own. But the masses who listened to King gradually swayed to the music of the black revolutionists.

Because the message of the black revolutionists is primarily for blacks and only indirectly for whites, the majority of Americans fail to understand the rhetoric. If the black rhetor has effect on whites then he has accomplished through language what he hoped to accomplish through black unity. Having seen the extensive camera coverage of the civil rights movement of the early 1960's, however, the black revolutionist is not unaware of his greater audience. Thus, the use of a circuitous strategy actually could be effective on the white audience. For example, the rhetor might open his address to a black audience with the television cameras recording the proceedings by suggesting that the blacks should consider burning down the white-owned businesses in the black ghetto.

Perhaps the white Americans could understand the rhetoric more readily if it was directly addressed to them. Unable to make an objective evaluation of a rhetoric that they seem to hear by chance, the majority of white Americans are confused and frightened by it. It is analogous to a man overhearing part of a conversation between persons next door about injuring him or his property. He is filled with intense anxiety because he cannot unravel the mystery that includes him in its center. But the black rhetor's message often affects those who overhear as much, though not in the same way, as those who hear directly.

In being receptive to the message, the black man discovered new awareness of and strength in his past by accepting his heritage and by understanding the slave. What the people of this audience could not do, and the black revolutionists told them they must not do, was to accept *slave-think.* Out of this refusal to accept *slave-think* evolved the black revolutionists' doctrine against the welfare system. They view the welfare system as deviously contributing to the undermining of black heritage, home, attitude, and dignity. Furthermore, the rhetoric suggests that the great dispenser of *slave-think* is the white American. Consequently, when blacks tried to gain their liberty and freedom in ways similar to those used by the early American revolutionaries, white Americans found it difficult to accept black assertiveness. In this connection, the black rhetors attempt to demonstrate that white Americans are not only involved in *slave-think* in America, but also deal in it in other parts of the world.

Favorite passages of the black rhetors cite the conspiratorial designs of the white man to assign *slave-think* to other peoples of the world. Usually the audience is prepared for the charge against the whites with an argumentative question, such as "Why did America drop the Bomb on Japan rather than Germany?" or, "Who installed Tshombe as leader of the Congo?" or, "Do you think America will fight for black liberation in South Africa?" The questions often are presented in a rhetorical way because for most black audiences the answers are self-evident. Answers are seldom given and explanations are not accepted; the assertion in the question becomes indictment enough.

Occasionally, a speaker or writer will allude to the paradox that occurred during World Wars I and II where blacks died for other people's rights, yet did not have those rights in their own land. Having prepared the audience for the contemporary situation, the black rhetor might end with the incisive retort, "If the white man plays Nazi, we ain't playing Jews."[16] Stokely Carmichael has made especially effective rhetorical use of this line for closing a speech. The statement has been used primarily by Carmichael and Brown, but lesser rhetors have joined the chant, thereby making what was a classic line worn and dull. I might

[16]Speech given by Stokely Carmichael to a Black Power Rally in South Park, Los Angeles, November 26, 1966.

remark here that the evolution of this retort is a good example of why there has been no truly eloquent black revolutionist since Malcolm X. Only Malcolm X spoke from the real convictions and experiences of life; there was nothing theatrical or sophistic about his rhetoric. That is not to say, however, that the other black revolutionists have not had real experiences and do not now have true convictions, but rather that they have not yet articulated their realities.

The black man's present susceptibility to the rhetoric of black revolution will be fully exposed only when the black forefathers are understood. Despite the hardships imposed upon them during and after slavery, these illiterate and semi-literate blacks told their children that times would be better. These are the people whom the black revolutionists, on cue from Malcolm X, have begun to vindicate. The field Negro, according to Malcolm X, never really gave up his manhood. In understanding this, it is fairly easy to see the children's need to witness those better times. Reconstruction merely remade the South into what it had been before the Civil War; only the names of processes, experiences, situations, and relationships were changed. Booker T. Washington captured the spirit of the new South by understanding that it was essentially the same South. After Washington, no black man stood so high in the public mind, until Dr. Martin Luther King, Jr.

If one were to give the requirements for a black charismatic leader, he could do little better than the life, experiences, education, and temperament of Martin Luther King, Jr. King was born in the South. He was the son of a Baptist preacher and was himself a preacher. Inasmuch as the vast majority of blacks in the South were active or nominal Baptists, this was a valuable asset. King could speak the language of the small town southern blacks when he invoked the prophets or the words of Jesus. Often speaking in the same melodious cadence black preachers had been using for years, King could captivate his audience by dropping the vocal pitch to give a sense of foreboding to the tone. He was the epitome of the black preacher.

History probably will record that he fulfilled a strategic mission in the black man's struggle for dignity, for after King's Montgomery encounter other rhetors using his style began appearing in cities having a large black population. If King could do it, they seemed to say, so can we. Even more important was the fact that even though he was educated, he could still speak the language of the small town preacher. There was a certain pride that ran through black communities whenever King was speaking or being interviewed on radio or television because he represented for many blacks the race at its best. There was a natural response to an educated Southern-born black man who spoke the language of the preachers. With the debut of Martin Luther King, Jr., a prophetic urgency gripped America as demonstrations of grievances were mounted throughout the nation. King and the Montgomery Improvement Association, which was later succeeded by the Southern Christian Leadership Conference, started a movement that would gain momentum with each succeeding year until finally it seemed to exhaust itself.

Only when the society did not appear to be responding to King's non-violent strategy did the black revolutionists seize the opportunity to preach self-assertiveness. Malcolm X said in the speech, "Message to the Grass Roots" on November 10, 1963, "When Martin Luther King failed to desegregate Albany, Georgia, the civil-rights struggle in America reached its low point. King became bankrupt, almost, as a leader."[17]

King's movement had been based on a fundamental belief in the goodness of man. He insisted that America had the moral courage to correct the injustices perpetrated on the black man. Beyond that, he believed that America would redress the grievances if those injustices were amply shown. With the extensive news coverage of the difficulties that blacks were having in getting accommodations, housing, and voting privileges, it was clear that America must now know what the black man faced. When the blacks of King's move-

[17]*Malcolm X Speaks*, p. 13.

ment had amply dramatized the situation, they hoped for an outburst of national indignation.

But with King's demonstrations, including pray-ins, ride-ins, sit-ins, and sleep-ins, America saw children pelted with rocks, students pulled from lunch counters, dogs unleashed by policemen on small children, and baseball bats brandished. With the deaths associated with the civil rights movement, the romanticism, partly induced by the rhetoric of Martin Luther King, Jr., turned sour. The demonstrators were greeted as outside agitators, disrupters of race relations, and lawbreakers. The expected reserve of national will to do what was right and honorable did not pay off in white America's consciences, although some important civil rights bills were passed by Congress.

Other than the blacks themselves, only idealistic white youth with a sense of national and personal will to correct years of injustices responded. Their response was visceral and genuine, and they too helped to create the "new black." It was their ideals and deeds of national concern that defined the magnitude of the problem. It was a realization of their impotence against what they called the establishment that convinced blacks like Stokely Carmichael of the need for a more radical means of persuasion.

The angry young blacks wished to take communication out of the realm of suggestion and put it into a more immediate and direct relationship. To do this, the black revolutionists insisted on alleviating the elements that kept the black masses helpless. Believing that enslavement can only be accomplished through force and superstition, the rhetors of black revolution attempted to liberate the black masses by using a militant rhetoric to change the black man's self-concept. With the emancipation of the slaves, force, for the most part, was eliminated as an instrument of slavery; but superstition continued to enslave the black man. The rhetoric seeks to deliver the black man from the humiliating image he has had of himself.

It is a rhetoric of exaggeration, to some extent, and that is another reason for its lack of total success. Black heritage and identity can be based on the true nature of African history without the obvious tall tales propagated by some nationalists and the Black Muslims. Elijah Muhammad taught his coterie of black nationalist preachers that a black scientist created the white man by mistake thousands of years ago. While the attempt by Muhammad's preachers to persuade the black masses never really succeeded, the exaggeration did teach the masses something about myth-making. Convinced that the white man had dominated other peoples of the world because his myths were stronger, the black rhetors saw an opportunity to re-direct and re-structure reality. An example of the re-structuring of reality with the black man at its center is the black revolutionist's description of his ethnic characteristics. Whereas most anthropological and sociological works by white authors describe the black man in comparison to the white man, the black revolutionists reverse the process. Their rhetoric suggests that compared to the black man, the average white man exhibits the following physical traits: head slightly less elegant, nose less well-developed, lips not so full, and hair stringy. The intent of this rhetoric is to get on the offensive by defining one's world in relationship to one's self, as indeed, the black revolutionists insist the white man has done for five hundred years.

With the emergence of the new black rhetoric in the late 1960's also came a refinement of the tools of protest speaking. The black revolutionists utilized the techniques of agitational rhetoric with a greater degree of sophistication than had Martin Luther King, Jr., Roy Wilkins, Bayard Rustin, or Whitney Young in their effort to liberate the black masses from superstition and white oppression.

Even though King's message did not contain the threat of violence committed by himself or his followers, the message of the black revolutionists was always "or else." The only times that King's rhetoric even hinted of violence were when he pleaded with America to accept his non-violent approach because rejection could only lead to violence. But he never intimated that he would be a party to or a preacher of violence. The message of Martin Luther King, Jr., was that of a preacher pleading with his congregation to repent of their sins lest evil times befall them. Calling America to higher purposes and seeking moral goals, King tried to persuade a whole nation of the beauty of justice, compassion, and love.

Where King's rhetoric was a request, the black revolutionists' is a demand. The black revolutionists warn that if their demands are not met, they have but one alternative for their complete freedom, violence. They employ few qualifiers in their language. They speak with certainty and directness about their intentions if the society fails to respond to their ultimatums. To show determination and promise, the black revolutionists often use "will" without modifiers. Instead of calling for moral understanding, the revolutionists say, "we will burn this town down if things do not change." But the phrase, "if things do not change" only appears to be an escape hatch. The black revolutionists usually are certain that things will ,not change, and they know that many in their audience will feel the same sense of futility. Of course, the directness and certainty of the language add to the rhetoric's dimension of urgency. The society is faced with a challenge from the black revolutionists, but at the same time the challengers are forced to make a decision. They cannot fail to "burn the town down," or "sack the corner grocery store" and still maintain their ethos in the black community. As an observation, it seems that those agitational movements that have repeatedly failed to produce actions comparable to their pronouncements have always been exhausted.

Furthermore, it is the strategy of the black revolutionists to particularize all grievances. In statements such as "No people has ever been denied free access to education and jobs like we have," "The Man consigns us, defines us and intimidates us, when other people would have died before they submitted," and "LBJ wants us to kill for them (whites), but if we kill, we gon' decide who we gon' kill," the aim is to get the audience to feel specifically persecuted by using words that isolate the hearers from others within the society.[18] Thus even with all of its aggressive characteristics, the rhetoric of black revolution is isolationistic. In search of definitions and limits, it seeks to carve out an area that the black audience can call its own. Whether in politics, art, music, language, or heroes, the task is to find a sphere sufficiently free of white intervention to call black.

But this is an essential paradox of the black revolutionists' rhetoric, that it cannot completely divorce itself from the white world. Ultimately, black revolutionary rhetoric is a creation of white society, for without the severities of white society the rhetoric would be unneeded. Even the Spirituals, which the black revolutionists rightly say were a black thing, were inspired by white oppression. Soul and all that it implies becomes a black thing in response to the white world.

Yet the constant goal of the black revolutionist is to occupy a moral or psychological territory that he can call his own. In the speeches made before black audiences, the attempt is made to stake out a position from which to charge the white society. It is both similar to and more than youth seeking to establish their own turfs and perimeters. Words are marshalled to canalize the opinions, beliefs, and emotions of the black masses into an offensive against the establishment.

You may have decided that the rhetoric possesses a militaristic outlook; indeed the style of the rhetoric does indicate reliance on military terminology. The rhetors have appropriated the language of revolution, whether revolution comes or not, to attain their rhetorical purpose. In the rhetoric of black revolution, sloganizing is nothing less than a form of rhetorical aggression. To state a complex or intricate concept in a few simple emotional words is effectively to agitate: WE WANT BLACK POWER; MOVE ON OVER OR WE WILL MOVE OVER YOU; HELL NO, WE WON'T GO. The rhetorical impact on the audience is related to the degree of assertiveness contained within the slogan. From the

[18]Carmichael, Los Angeles, November 26, 1966.

slogans, society tends to acquire impressions of the revolutionists as "militant," "violent," "belligerent," "self-assertive," or "dominating." The actions of the rhetors may not be violent, although their followers may react to their speeches by engaging in violence. But the stigma of militancy or being violent is not necessarily dependent on physical actions. Primarily, it is in the use of language that the rhetor of revolution becomes identified as militant. In much the same way as a slogan's degree of assertiveness affects the society by causing people to form impressions of the sloganizer, the intensity of the assertion also figures in a slogan's ability to galvanize a given audience. However, the more assertive a slogan is, the fewer its adherents. Some people who accepted WE SHALL OVERCOME could not subsequently shout WE WANT BLACK POWER or MOVE ON OVER OR WE WILL MOVE OVER YOU. The last slogan contains the agitational or that suggests an alternative unfavorable to the agitator's opposition. As a rhetorical device, it contains a threat of violence, and therefore must be considered an emotional addition to the linguistic composition of a rhetorical discourse. Thus the slogan becomes what it was originally as a Scottish war cry—a call to militancy.

In the volatile context of social relationships, changing mores, interrelated and unrelated life patterns, the stage is prepared for the black revolutionist who exploits the inadequacies of the social system. The black masses may see the system as anything from the weekly service bills to the inability of a parent to supply a child with lunch money. The system is even more violent because of their blackness. Where others may speak of social slights or stupid prejudices of white America, the revolutionists see everything in terms of a design to undermine the dignity of black people.

The revolutionist exploits the black masses' belief that the white man's system is evil; he also dwells on the disillusionment caused by that system. The theme of disaffection with America is prevalent in the rhetoric of the black revolutionist. It is present in such statements as, "What do we have to lose if the country is burned down," and "America has always been racist and has always given us a bad deal," and, "we should be fighting in South Carolina rather than in South Vietnam."[19]

Commonly, the rhetor of this rhetoric uses the chronological pattern of organization to bring his audience up to the present time on racial matters. Once this is accomplished, he usually asks his audience "Now, what has America done for you?" The black audiences immediately make a negative mental response to the question. Capitalizing on the various military campaigns the black American has fought in, the revolutionist wants to know, Why give your life for the yellow man's freedom when you don't have your own? By his affirmations, the black revolutionist thus strengthens the masses' disillusionment with white society. The rhetorical context, then, is one of diverse social and moral patterns that allow the black revolutionists the opportunity to exploit the grievances of the masses, whether political, social, economic or cultural.

Suggested Readings

For background information on the Civil Rights Movement, see Louis Lomax, *The Negro Revolt*, New York, 1962. A perceptive analysis of the American racial situation can be found in Charles Silberman, *Crisis in Black and White*, New York, 1964. C. Eric Lincoln, *My Face is Black*, Boston, 1964, is an excellent treatment of the black man's history of protest in America. See also Kenneth B. Clark, *Dark Ghetto: Dilemmas of Social Power*, New York, 1965, for an interpretation of black attitudes based on research with the Haryou program in Harlem.

For materials on the revolutionary thinking in the black community, see Lewis M. Killian, *The Impossible Revolution?*, New York, 1968. Although Killian insists that there is no way out of the

[19]Carmichael, Los Angeles, November 26, 1966.

racial situation, his interpretation of black awareness and black power is clear and concise. Perhaps the best statement on the black man's desperation and reason for it is William H. Grier and Price M. Cobbs, *Black Rage*, New York, 1968. Two black psychiatrists explain the detrimental effects of the slave experience for black Americans. See also George S. Pettee, *The Process of Revolution*, New York, 1938; and Frantz Fanon, *The Wretched of the Earth*, New York, 1968.

2
Strategies of the Revolutionists

The black revolutionist is essentially an agitator in that he persistently challenges the power complex to effect a dramatic situational change, such as a change in the balance of power, a redefining of the goal of American Democracy, or drastic alterations in the Constitution. In response to the black revolutionist's demands, the white community, sensing a rhetoric that intends to alter the *status quo*, seeks expurgation in yelling 'outside agitator.' Although it is true that every community in America where there are black people is potentially confronted with agitators, to say 'outside agitator' in the midst of revolutionists' demands is to convince one's self that before rabble-rousers moved in all was well.

But the term outside agitator is usually no more than a demeaning stereotype to stigmatize a spokesman for equality, dignity, human respect, and justice. In the following discussion, I will submit that the black revolutionist is an agitator because he employs stylistic strategies particularly appropriate to the terrifying and unifying characteristics of his rhetoric.

It is clear that because the agitator's purpose is different from the statesman's, for example, he necessarily uses rhetorical designs peculiar to his ends. His designs are peculiar not in the sense that he lacks the traditional rhetorical tools, such as invention, arrangement, style, and

25

delivery, but that he utilizes specialized designs within these conventional canons. For instance, the agitator's rhetorical style is less ordered and elegant, but more caustic and direct than the statesman's style. Furthermore, the statesman will usually speak with an even-tempered vocal delivery, whereas the agitator may speak in short, staccato sentences. The differences between a Dennis Kearney and a Henry George or an H. "Rap" Brown and a Martin Luther King, Jr., are due as much to the choice of rhetorical strategies as to rhetorical content; indeed, they are interrelated. Within the category of style, there are numerous rhetorical possibilities, each, of course, dependent on the rhetor's aim. Therefore, when I discuss the rhetoric of the black revolution in an effort to ascertain the peculiar characteristics and appeals of that movement, I must define strategies consistent with the rhetor's goal.

The special rhetorical strategies that emerge from analyses of revolutionary rhetoric, political or social, are (1) vilification, (2) objectification, (3) legitimation, and (4) mythication.[1] These agitational devices, although not always consciously contrived in an agitator's rhetoric, are the logical extensions of his rhetorical aim. I have already stated the concepts of terror and unity present within an agitation; thus, when the agitator's goal is to accomplish a dramatic situational change in the society, it will follow that the above devices, contrived or not, will be present within his rhetoric.

Vilification is the agitator's use of language to degrade an opponent's person, actions, or ideas. When the agitator speaks of former vice-president Humphrey as a "political chameleon," or of former president Johnson as a "buffoon," he is engaging in vilification.[2] Unlike invective, which is usually applicable to one or several people, vilification is always concerned with using caustic and bitter language

[1] See Arthur L. Smith, Jr., *Samuel Adams' Agitational Rhetoric of Revolution*, unpublished dissertation (UCLA, 1968), for a detailed discussion of agitational strategies.

[2] Charles Lomas, *The Agitator in American Society*, Englewood, New Jersey, 1968, pp. 137–151.

against one person. The person vilified is usually well-known to the audience; indeed, it is the dynamic of the strategy that the audience can identify the person vilified as a leader of the opposition. Thus, vilification is almost always directed toward a conspicuous leader of the opposition rather than toward an unknown personality.

By calling the name of the anti-hero, the agitator presents the audience with an opportunity for catharsis. The immediate end of the strategy appears to be an audience reaction of contempt toward the person vilified. Because popularity and unpopularity rest with the beholders, the agitator's vilification function is to get the audience to disprove of the representative of the opposition. This is mainly accomplished by exposing corruptions, inefficiencies, lies, intrigues, and injustices. Whether the agitator supports his charges with valid data at the moment of utterance is apparently irrelevant, although ultimately his cause might be affected by his lack of facts. But a major part of vilification is indictment of the conspicuous leader; the agitator might even allow the audience to make its own decision as to whether or not the president is a buffoon.

The choice of the opposition leader to be vilified, similar to the choice of language, is a rhetorical decision for the agitator. The black revolutionist is interested in vilifying a person who has been publicized enough for the black masses to know, and perhaps despise. There is little danger of a rhetorical failure if the agitator can stake out a conspicuous leader of the opposition who is already held in low esteem in the community. This means that the President of the United States and his cabinet are the most suitable persons to vilify when a rhetor is commenting on problems of national concern. In this case, the mayor of Uvalde, Texas, or Valdosta, Georgia, would be an inappropriate target of the agitator's rhetoric. However, within those communities, the mayors could conceivably be the most conspicuous leaders for a divergent view and would then be appropriate persons for agitators to vilify. A general rule of vilification might well be that the agitator vilifies a conspicuous leader where he is known, never where he is unknown, unless by example.

The rhetoric of black revolution mainly utilizes political persons for vilification. Those who have been elected or appointed to serve in a public position are vulnerable to attack because of their visibility. Physicians, accountants, and businessmen may be as strongly opposed to the revolutionist's point of view as is the politician, but they are not nearly as suitable for vilification because of their low visibility. Therefore, men such as former president Johnson, Robert McNamara, Dean Rusk, Ramsey Clark, Ronald Reagan, Richard Nixon, and Barry Goldwater become the vilified by the agitator because of their national publicity.

The rhetor often employs language highly charged with emotional content when referring to the person vilified. Uncompromising statements and bitter denunciations are generally used to provoke the opposition into more open combat. Agitation depends on active opposition for its success, because only with massive and intense opposition can the inactive masses see the clear outline of the situation. The agitator believes that he is more likely to bring about a dramatic situational change if he meets with opposition because the masses will join his cause. Sometimes the creation of the opposition becomes a task of the agitator when negative reaction is lacking toward his position.

A lack of active opposition, however, usually indicates weakness in the agitator's campaign because it says that the community is indifferent to the agitator. Actually, a meaningful agitation is only developed when the *status quo* rises to block the creation of sentiments favorable to the agitator. Once this occurs, the agitator is able to point to one of the chief figures of the opposition as the epitome of what should be rejected, hated, despised, and condemned.

Vilification, then, is the use of harsh language against a single conspicuous leader of the opposition with the intent of belittling him before the community. By vilifying the opposition's chief figure, the agitator seeks to degrade those who resist his movement. This strategy employs sarcasm, low humor, re-interpretation of words or actions, and the making of overt charges. Clearly, vilification is the agitator's most personal attack on his opposition.

Another stratagem which is employed by the black agitator is _objectification_. It is the agitator's use of language to direct the grievances of a particular group toward another collective body such as an institution, nation, political party, or race. Related to, but differing from vilification, objectification uses similar devices of sarcasm and low humor while attacking an ill-defined body. Both strategies direct attention to the opposition, and both seek to embarrass the opposition; however, objectification strives to channel all of the frustrations of a group onto a single ill-defined body.

The agitator is concerned with showing that a certain race, party, or secret collection of men is responsible for all of the misfortune that befalls the agitator's votarists. The solution is simple: we must get rid of them. The notorious Hitlerian rhetoric of the German Third Reich is a classic example of this strategy, which has been employed by rhetors of every age and for various causes throughout history. It has been used both as a repressive strategy to maltreat one group and as a revolutionary strategy to overthrow a dominant or ruling group. No effort is made to single out any member of the group, but rather to concentrate on the collection of individuals. The groups become 'dirty Jews,' 'Yankees,' 'Crackers,' 'honkies,' 'Illuminati,' 'Niggers' and so forth, to the agitators who blame the groups for all of the difficulties of their followers.

Objectification provides the agitator with greater protection from scrutiny. Because his attacks are directed toward an ill-defined group, it is almost impossible to make an exacting examination. Another reason that objectification is a safer strategy for the agitator than is vilification is inherent in the relatively stable nature of ill-defined bodies. Although an individual may represent the opposition only temporarily due to term of office, pleasure of an executive, or death, the collective object of an agitator's attacks is little affected by the opposition's personnel changes. Inasmuch as agitation proceeds on the basis of grievances deeply felt, those grievances are usually not changed by the retirement of a political official; this is especially true if the agitator has concentrated on objectification rather than on vilification. If the agitator assigns all of the grievances and frustrations of his followers to a single person, he is liable to be in business only at the will of the opposition.

For example, during the agitational campaign of the American Revolution, Governor Bernard was heavily attacked with stinging denunciation by James Otis and Samuel Adams.[3] In August, 1768, King George III recalled Bernard to London. If the agitators had made Bernard the total object of their hatreds, then when he left, the agitation would have lost its source. But because Adams had attacked the "cursed Cabal" as the despicable source of the colonists' problems, no face was lost when Bernard returned to England.[4] Indeed, Bernard may have been among those Adams collectively called "Cabal"; but when the governor left, the "Cabal" remained. Thus, because objectification is the canalization of a group's negative feeling toward a collective body as the source of grievances, it never singles out individuals, as does vilification.

In the black revolution, the justificatory rhetoric has utilized objectification many times and with varying degrees of effectiveness. When the revolutionist shouts that the "white power structure of America has begun its slide into the darkness of cheap obscurity because it has been a power structure of race hatred," he is employing the technique of objectification.[5] So is any radical newspaper that proclaims that the blackman's struggle is against "Whitey."

[3]Francis Bernard succeeded Thomas Pownall as governor of the Massachusetts Bay Colony in 1760. During his administration, the Boston radicals, led by Samuel Adams and James Otis, caused considerable turmoil in Massachusetts politics. The agitation, demonstrations, and riots of the Sons of Liberty and other malcontents finally forced King George to recall Bernard.

[4]Boston Gazette, October 2, 1769.

[5]Speech given by Stokely Carmichael in South Park, Los Angeles, California, November 26, 1966.

The use of objectification as an agitational strategy usually depends on the agitator's ability to seize the offensive. The suspicion that aggression is present on this level becomes a reality when we see how the black revolutionist often seems deliberately to choose militant words and expressions, such as 'fight', 'put out of action', 'neutralize', and 'move against' to convey the movement's intentions.

Blame is apparently the overriding element in the dynamics of objectification. The rhetor must lure the opposition into position, if it is not already there, for blame. If the opposition is especially vulnerable because of past actions and views, then the agitator has only to make his charges. However, if the opposition is not so vulnerable as to be a favorable target for the agitator, then the opposition is usually lured into position by provocative statements or actions by the agitator's followers. It is not always necessary, however, as recent civil and college campus confrontations have shown, for the agitator's followers to provoke the opposition; they have only to threaten a provocation and often the opposition, which usually represents the *status quo*, responds vigorously. Blaming the ill-defined body is a rhetorical aggression meant to put the opposition out of action by causing it to spend time defending its views and actions. Once this is accomplished, the agitator can move on to other areas of confrontation with the intention of demonstrating the inadequacy of the *status quo*.

In his use of objectification, the black revolutionist's aim is to make coherent the numerous social and political grievances within the black community. To seek some explanations, to draw some conclusions for the deprived masses, the black revolutionist turns to the elementary.

It is important to remember that whether the charges or the grievances are true at the outset of an agitational campaign is irrelevant. Only one thing is significant to the revolutionist, and by him, to the masses, and that is what are the reasons for black suffering. Even though it matters greatly whether the charges or grievances are true for the ultimate strength of the agitation, agitations are often made on what people believe reality to be.

It is true that traditionally the black rhetor has had just cause for complaint. From economic deprivations to subtle discriminatory actions, the black man has undergone the tragedy of his American experience. Thus, when the black revolutionist responds to the black man's plight with whitey or white power structure or simply the Man, the audience apparently receives a rewarding relief. A relief not so much because others have been blamed (and yet in part because of this) but because the masses have at last pointed the accusing finger at the Man. The fact that someone has been blamed is significant, but even more significant is the fact that the powerless have done the blaming.

I submit in this connection that the agitator who best produces in the gathered masses the necessary catharsis to relieve them of their despair becomes for them the leader. Objectification suggests opposites, or at least the blamed and the blamers; and the leader of a mass agitation must be able effectively to enlarge the distance between his group and the hated group. He must not only identify but also affix blame to the enemy. Blame becomes the expression of a collective despair turned against those in the society who possess means to eradicate the alleged causes of grievances or who should be removed from positions of authority so that the agitational ends are accomplished.

It should be clear from this discussion that objectification can serve to create a mass leader. In agitational campaigns, the leader usually emerges from the masses because of his vociferous denunciations of the opposition. This seems to suggest that the person who can best express the desires of the masses in regard to the opposition can be expected to attain a significant following.

Heightening the rhetorical effectiveness in objectification is achieved by the use of derogatory names or titles. For this reason the term whitey is more potent than white power structure, and the racist honky government excites more passions than does the phrase white government. Similarly, to refer to the police as pigs is more derogatory objectification than is racist police force. The skillful agitator or demagogue is able to appropriate the most current terms to his campaign. And too, there seems to be a certain aura that surrounds the creator of a term for the opposition to which the masses are responsive. Creation of terms degrading to the opposition allows the leader to demonstrate the currency of his thinking.

However, to continue to be effective, the agitator must be careful not to use derisive language that is not sanctioned by his followers. One can almost trace the masses' disaffection with Stokely Carmichael to the time when he got hard on the honkies. This is not to say that Carmichael did not have a strong following after his hard line; but his following became much smaller. Many of the middle-class blacks who accepted his self-help, self-dignity, and even black power philosophy could not see themselves accepting his name-calling tactics.

When addressing a black audience, the agitator must consider the predominantly religious nature of the group. Even though many blacks are only nominally Christian, there is an emphasis on the authoritarian as exemplified by many black preachers in their sermons. When the agitator can create in precise terms the enemy as the masses observe him in their own realities, he becomes in effect a preacher. Thus, the use of language to channel the grievances of the group onto an ill-defined body can give the agitator influence similar to that exercised by black preachers.

As the black preacher often cites scriptural references to support a statement or to substantiate a definition, the secular-agitator-become-preacher also often refers to specific events or incidents to indict his opposition or to prove his charge. He effects the rhetorical techniques of the preacher and other persuaders as he endeavors to convince the masses that his definitions of the opposition as honkies and whiteys are valid. Having succeeded in persuading his audience to the extent that they respond to the external world on the basis of his views, the agitator has accomplished objectification. He has put an ill-defined collective symbol before the minds of his followers in order to get them to react against the opposition, and their response becomes indicative of the efficacy of his agitation.

As important to an agitational movement as vilification and objectification is the strategy of *mythication*. Employing language that suggests the sanction of supra-rational forces, the agitator creates a spiritual dynamism for his movement. Seizing on what is probably the rationale for black hope, the agitator often attempts to use religious symbolism in an' effort to demonstrate the righteousness of his cause.

Religious symbolism creates for the black masses a needed escape from the pressures of a predominantly white' society that relegates them to a second-class citizenship. The black agitator can be extremely influential when appealing to 'God of Abraham, Isaac, and Jacob', or more basically, to 'the God of Israel'. Significantly, black preachers have used the Israelitic pilgrimage in nearly every possible way. According to the black rhetors, the blacks, like the Jews, have suffered oppression; like the Jews, they have often been persecuted; and like the Jews they cannot "sing a new song in a strange land."[6]

And yet, despite this reluctance to sing a new song, the older more soulful songs of the slave era do find expression in black communities. To some degree, there is in black ghettoes, North and South, the music of the children of Israel. Songs such as "Go down Moses, Way down in Egypt's Land," "Daniel in the Lion's Den," and "Joshua Fit the Battle of Jericho" are still heard in choral groups. Out of this music and the accompanying theology there developed a messianic-like hope on the part of black Americans. After slavery, it was only beginning to be intensified when the black man felt the pinches of new clasps.

Many black parents named their children Moses, Aaron, or David after Israel's heroes, and still do in some remote parts of the South. This tradition reflects a deep wishing for the equals of those ancient Israelites to spring up in the black community. Moses and David were the names most used from the Old Testament. In Moses, the black

[6]Psalms 137:4.

masses had great psychological power for no one could defeat the people who dreamed of Moses.

In many ways, Langston Hughes' song of the "Dream Deferred" had little applicability to this phenomenon. Whereas the reality of equality was a long ways off, the dream of Moses was a reality alive within the hearts of the people. In another sense, the dreams were not the same.

The dream of black and white together in the American society was considered unrealizable within the lifetimes of those black mothers and fathers who named their sons Moses. Those parents often told their children that the dream would not be realized in their life spans, but that it was destined to be reality for the children. Their vision was of a Moses, both a theological and political happening, who would deliver the oppressed masses. Thus, the messianic-like hope helped to ease the pains of economic and political misery.

Perhaps it is significant that only in the last few years has the black man intensely felt the "coming of the Lord," as Martin Luther King, Jr., expressed it in a Memphis church in April, 1968, shortly before his assassination. To King, as to many other black rhetors, there was something social in the biblical expression, 'I have seen the glory of the coming of the Lord.'

The rhetoric employed by black agitators since David Walker may have come to fruition in the language and style of a black preacher born in the South and educated in the North. With Martin Luther King, Jr., the black man no longer refused to speak up for his rights and no longer bowed in submission to the white man's orders. During the Montgomery bus boycott, there was much talk of the new Negro, and books were written to explain this novel development in American society.[7]

While King, perhaps more than anyone else, was the embodiment of black hope and determination as rep-

[7]See particularly Louis E. Lomax, *The Negro Revolt*, New York, 1962; and James Baldwin, *The Fire Next Time*, New York, 1962.

resented in religious symbolism, he was by no means the only black leader so perceived. And it seems that the black masses who gathered around King during the early days of his movement felt isolated during the latter stages. Apparently, King's strength with the black masses, especially in the South, lay with his strong appeal to the religious precepts, principles, and ideals of the black Baptists and other fundamentalists in the South. Once he left the source of his wide popular appeal and more ardently became a disciple of Mahatma Gandhi, many of the blacks, reared in a fundamental Christian environment, could accept neither his intellectualism nor his mysticism. They had been converted by his early rhetoric, which possessed themes that they readily comprehended. During King's career, and especially after he received the Nobel Peace Prize, his rhetoric broadened to include all of the oppressed peoples of the world. In fact, he became the conscience for many people. Among his legacies is an unswerving indictment of all that he considered unjust and detrimental to the human spirit. What King also did for the black man in America was to dramatize the possibility of overcoming the forces of evil with united action.

But mythication uses history itself as an instrument of its aim. The black rhetor wants to demonstrate that his agitation is sanctioned by history because great agitations have sought to establish justice, create equality, and build dignity. The rhetors of black revolution emphasize that "history is on our side," "truth will win out in the end," and "just causes seldom fail."[8] The appropriation of the combined forces of the universe on the side of the black revolution is the black revolutionist's demonstration of mythication.

In using mythication, the rhetor is primarily concerned with his immediate audience and only indirectly with the wider audience. That is, the mythication strategy functions as a sanction for the followers of a movement by assigning

[8]Speech given by Minister Franklin Florence at Purdue University, October, 1968.

supra-rational support to their beliefs, actions, and goals. The agitator gives the audience a faith in order to capture their imaginations as well as their bodies. This strategy is primarily exhortative in the sense that it becomes a type of group self-congratulation by the agitator in order to inspire them to greater dedication. It is identifiable in the written and oral discourse of the black revolutionists by appeals to God, posterity, history, the race, forefathers, destiny, and so forth.

By suggesting that "it is our destiny," "the flow of history dictates," or this plan is good for "our children," the rhetor effects an exhortation for his audience. The audience is connected to the great universe; and in this situation it matters little how small or ineffective the group is seen by the larger world. The group possesses a spiritual dynamism that sets it off from all other groups because of the appropriation of certain supra-rational influences to its cause. The members of the group become for all practical reasons the chosen people, the saviors, and the beautiful. They recognize the peculiar challenge confronting them as a group if the rhetor speaks to them in terms of forefathers and posterity. Indeed, the group often feels that it must perform the planned task, and it alone. Thus, the black revolutionists are careful to develop a sense of selectivity among their followers.

To struggle against the opposition, the group must not become one with the opposition; its identity must remain separate. When the distinctions between the agitational movement and the opposition no longer exist, an agitation is no longer relevant. The distinctions between the black revolutionists and the opposition are most dramatically set forth in the black nationalist's land demand. At once the vision of Israel coming out of corrupt Egypt appears. The black revolutionist quotes, "And the Lord said, Come ye out from among them."[9] Thus even in this seemingly secular demand is a religious possibility for the black masses.

Black nationalist groups have a long tradition of seek-

[9] II Corinthians 6:17.

ing this most dramatic division with the status quo. Paul Cuffee, a black New England sailor, sent nearly forty black colonists to Africa in 1815.[10] Dr. Martin Delaney, editor of a Pittsburgh weekly newspaper, *The Mystery*, secured permission from several kings in the Niger Valley to ship black emigrants in 1858. And in the early 1920's, Marcus Garvey roared across the American stage with a powerful message of black pride and unity. He called on black men to forget equality in America and to seek freedom on the continent of Africa.

After Garvey's enthusiastic movement failed because of poor business management by his associates, he was imprisoned for defrauding by mail. C. Eric Lincoln in *The Black Muslims in America* contends that Garvey was betrayed by the black intellectuals who considered Garvey's Universal Negro Improvement Association dangerous to their positions in American society. Thus they cried, "Garvey must go!"[11] Finally, after serving four years in the Federal penitentiary in Atlanta, Garvey was pardoned and deported in 1927; he died in London in 1940.

In 1930, Wallace D. Fard, claiming to be a prophet, began calling for black separatism. Fard's idea, unlike that of most of his nationalist predecessors, was for black people to have a land carved from the United States. He argued that black Americans had been "surrounded and robbed completely by the cave man." Using such terms for the white man as 'satan,' 'devil,' and 'cave man,' Fard refined the distinctions between white America and black America.[12] His rhetoric gave his followers a reason for self-compliments.

Directly out of Fard's movement came the Nation of Islam or Black Muslim religious sect started in 1933. The Nation of Islam still preaches that the black masses or so-called Negroes must unite and separate from white America because the time for America's destruction is at hand. Al-

---

[10]See E. U. Essien-Udom, *Black Nationalism*, New York, 1964, for a comprehensive view of early black nationalism movements.
[11]C. Eric Lincoln, *The Black Muslims in America*, Boston, 1961, p. 64.
[12]*Ibid.*, pp. 10–12.

though this sect provides the black man with reasons for self-congratulation, it has never convinced large numbers of black Americans that separation is the solution to their predicament. The Black Muslims have never really understood their failure to communicate to the black masses. While it is true that the black American has been brainwashed by an overpowering white culture, it is also true that the Black Muslims' rhetoric cannot undo that brainwashing as it is now stated. One reason that Malcolm X appealed to large numbers of blacks was his ability to separate the dogmatics of the Black Muslim religion from what he called its political philosophy.

But for the most part, the Black Muslims have tried to convince black people, who are essentially Christian in their outlook, to accept religious views that are strange and often contradictory to their Christian heritage. As a technique of mythication, the Black Muslims' appeal to history for support of their concept of race superiority seeks to provide the oppressed masses with reason to fight.

Most of the current black revolutionists are not persuaded by the Black Muslims' religious rhetoric, but find their strength in the theme of blackness. They see the question of religion as irrelevant to their task. "We are here and we want part of the action, or there ain't going to be no action,"[13] a black revolutionist shouted to a cheering throng. Whereas the Black Muslims have made the superiority of the black man a major tenet of their religious dogma by suggesting that an evil black scientist created the white man, the black revolutionists often view the Black Muslims as having the "same ole hang-up with religion and superstition."[14]

The present situation is important to the black revolutionist as it exists for the blacks in the ghettoes and in the rural South. His theme is the glorification of the black man

---

[13]Speech given by Stokely Carmichael in South Park, Los Angeles, California, November 26, 1966.

[14]Interview with Bob Jones, black student leader, Purdue University, November, 1968.

apart from religion; it is in this sense that he sees the black man's mission for an American renewal. "Black is beautiful" becomes the myth that calls the black American to work out his destiny. According to the black revolutionist, it is necessary to develop pride in one's heritage before unity can be achieved against the forces of oppression. Thus, the black revolutionist campaigns against skin brighteners and hair straighteners in his effort to create ownness in the black American. Attempting to instill new dignity, he speaks in favor of naturals, soul food, jazz, and even drums as methods of black assertiveness. More than anything else, the black revolutionist is an exhorter as he insists that black is beautiful and better.

What becomes clear in this discussion of mythication is that it always operates for a specific group that can be defined to the exclusion of others. The rhetor who employs mythication gives his audience a feeling of particularity. However, inasmuch as mythication sanctions and directs the aspirations of a people, only a rhetoric that employs symbolisms and images larger than any segment of the nation's population can bring about national unity.

Finally, the rhetor of black revolution makes use of *legitimation*. Insofar as it is the use of language to answer the opposition, it is a refutative strategy. But it is more than an argumentative rebuttal to an opponent; it is a psychological weapon. In legitimation, the black revolutionist seeks to explain, vindicate, and justify the activists involved in his movement. Affecting his attitude, outlook, and possibilities, the technique of mythication is vital to the revolutionist's campaign, especially if it is inclined toward activism. It is here, then, in activism, that legitimation is distinguished.

Aggression is a main characteristic of revolutionary rhetoric, for only by taking the offensive can the agitator succeed in convincing the masses of the viability of his solutions. In this connection, legitimation becomes essential to the momentum and inspiration of the movement. As a justificatory design, it explains whatever actions occur at the hands of activists as resulting from the opposition's

arrogance or obstinacy. Historically, it has made little difference to revolutionists whether their friends engaged in
burning and looting colonial Boston, emptying private tea
into the harbor, or setting fires to liquor stores in the black
ghettoes, so long as the activists did it for the cause. Indeed,
after the conflagrations in Watts, Detroit, and Newark, the
black revolutionists explained that the buildings were
burned down because the people were tired of oppression
and discrimination. Squirming to evade the charges of riot
and hooliganism, the agitator defines the actions as a
rebellion or a revolution. If grocery stores, furniture stores,
and liquor stores are looted, it is because the people have
lost many dollars of hard-earned money on poor products
or by paying exorbitant prices. Thus the agitator does not
allow himself to be encapsulated by the charges of his opposition.

Immediately after the activists launch their attacks, the
agitator is explaining the action as a response that never
would have occurred had the opposition listened. Legitimation becomes the imputing of wrong attitudes to the opposition even while the activists are attacking that very
opposition. Samuel Adams demonstrated this strategy in
colonial America when the Boston mob ransacked the
town.

In contemporary times, after major riots in several
cities, the black rhetors of revolution have explained the
nature of the conditions that provoked the violent reactions.
Violence was not planned; it was provoked and thus grew
directly out of oppressive conditions. Whenever a rhetor
vindicates the persons engaged in violent activism, he is
using the strategy of legitimation. As a rhetorical tool, legitimation reverses the charges against the votarists. Instead of
defending, the rhetor legitimizes by making counter-charges
against his accusers.

Clearly, the black revolutionist as agitator employs
language that has the characteristics of vilification, objectification, mythication, and legitimation. He endeavors to degrade and stigmatize the opposition with the strategies of

vilification and objectification; and he attempts to unify and defend his followers with mythication and legitimation. Even though these strategies are not necessarily found in all agitational rhetoric in the same degree, they always occur at some point in an agitational campaign waged with intensity and persistence.

Suggested Readings

Charles Lomas, *The Agitator in American Society*, Englewood, New Jersey, 1968, is one of the best recent works on agitation. Of particular importance is the chapter on the nature of agitation. Lomas provides a rubric for the critical evaluation of agitation speaking.

For an in depth view of black nationalism, see E. U. Essien-Udom, *Black Nationalism: A Search for an Identity in America*, Chicago, 1962; also C. Eric Lincoln, *The Black Muslims in America*, Boston, 1961. Lincoln's work is a penetrating look at the rise and growth of the Black Muslims in America. See also Louis E. Lomax, *When the Word is Given: A Report on Elijah Muhammad, Malcolm X, and the Black Muslim World*, Cleveland, 1963.

Stokely Carmichael and Charles Hamilton, *Black Power: Politics of Liberation in America*, New York, 1967, is a serious presentation of the black power philosophy. For further reading on the black power philosophy, see Floyd B. Barbour, ed., *The Black Power Revolt*, Boston, 1968. This is an excellent collection of essays on the subject. See also George Breitman, *The Last Year of Malcolm X*, New York, 1967; and Roy Hill, *The Rhetoric of Racial Revolt*, Denver, 1964.

3

Topics of Revolutionary Rhetoric

Having alluded to the black revolutionists' ideas in my discussion of situation and strategies (see Chapter 2), I now turn into an exposition of the rhetorical topics and themes.

In part, many rhetorical themes propagated by the contemporary black revolutionists have their source in the religious traditions of the slaves.[1] White justification for the importation of slaves during the era of black slavery often took the form of religious sanction. Self-congratulatory whites told themselves that by introducing Christianity to the slaves, they were civilizing the African savages. Many blacks, seeking a heavenly solace, believed and accepted the white man's religion with passionate zeal and accompanying emotionalism. When the social demands of slavery caused the black converts who had worshipped in their masters' churches to be segregated, small meeting places were built on the plantation for the slaves. These church houses, usually located on the edge of the plantation, were the centers of social and religious gatherings for blacks. During slavery, black preachers galvanized the members of the plantation churches with long moanful intonations of the

---

[1] For a more comprehensive view of Afro-American religion, see William E. B. Du Bois, *The Negro Church*, Atlanta, 1903; Mark Fisher, *Negro Slave Songs in the United States*, Ithaca, 1953; and Carter G. Woodson, *The History of the Negro Church*, Washington, 1921.

sufferings of the children of Israel. These slave preachers exercised considerable influence over their congregations because of their position of leadership, which suggested superior abilities and gifts. It is little wonder that Denmark Vesey and Nat Turner could command followers when it is revealed that they were both preachers. Thus, the black preacher was in a unique position that could be used either to compromise the longings of his congregation or to lead a revolt.

Realizing the power of the black preacher over his congregation, the slave owners often rewarded with household goods the preachers who performed well. In many instances, the black preachers became informers, pimps, and justifiers of slavery. Using the material gifts to the preacher, the white slave owner continued his domination of his slaves and put the minister in debt to the master.

The unique position of the black preacher also gave him the opportunity to organize and incite rebellions. Because the preacher had a direct path to the master and a direct path to God, he became the leader of the black community. Black preachers were reserved a special place in the community because they were 'in with the man.' In this position, the black preacher could get favors that other slaves could not acquire in their non-ministerial capacities. There might be a connection between the preacher's ability to secure special privileges from 'the man' and the fact that in many small Southern communities there is still an abundance of preachers. By allowing the master an opportunity to control the masses through the preacher, Christianity proved to be a powerful force; but it was later to figure in the black man's liberation and continuing struggle against discrimination and prejudice. This became inevitable when black preachers who were 'in with the man' used their knowledge to aid their congregations. They developed a thematic emphasis that indicated their concern about their parishioners.

It was not enough for the black preacher to bring gifts from the master to the slaves; he had to comfort them in their destitution by pointing to a heavenly reward for good living. In this role, the black preacher perfected the art of inducing cathartic experiences for his members. Indeed after some sermons, members of the audience were prostrate on the floor with foam running out of their mouths. The business of the black preacher during slavery was the business of consolation. He consoled in life as well as in death, for life was often a living death. He also developed a strong imagination to go with his ministerial functions. It is from this imagination that the black preacher received his special 'revelations' on certain scriptural themes.

As with the spirituals, the black preacher's sermons were often cryptic, suggesting more than they purported to say on the surface, thereby providing a deeper temporal meaning for the audience. In some church circles within the black community even now when a preacher touches on a theme with ambiguous meaning, church members might respond, "that's deep." Often when the slaves sang as they worked in the fields, "Swing Low, Sweet Chariot, Coming for to Take me Home," they were sending messages to one another; for example, "If you Get there Before I do, Tell All My Friends I'm Coming too," suggested that their escape was being planned. Other spirituals contained similar messages. The black preacher, similarly, gave out texts from the pulpit that contained dual meanings, "one for the spirit, and one for the body." In many places in the South today, some sermons with dual meanings are still heard. A favorite among black preachers during slavery, and still preached in the deep South is, "The Eagle Stirreth Her Nest," which suggested that the slaves were restive and ready for an uprising. The black preacher was the instrument through whom the 'message' of the Lord came to bring consolation and advice to the slaves.

Out of this context came the black rhetors basic reliance on Biblical concepts for the black man's liberation. Observing in the Old Testament the dramatic pronouncements made by the prophets Amos, Micah, and Jeremiah, the black preacher became a prophet. Among the themes that permeated the sermons were the broad concepts of justice, righteousness, and truth. Black preachers used these religious abstractions in much the same way as politicians employ the political abstractions. Justice, in the Old Testament, seems to be a major concern of the Israelitic prophets, and black preachers have traditionally found their texts in the prophets. The early Christian writers have had less influence on the black church, because the sufferings of the early Christians were not perceived as being parallel to that of black people. In Israel's deliverance from bondage and subsequent struggle to remain free, the black preacher found reason to moralize and counsel. It is the justice of God working its way out for an eternal good, according to the black preacher who explained the distress of black people whose parents were tortured and whose own lives were wretched with misery. Often in describing the aspirations of the black masses, the preachers would suggest that our way is "the way of righteousness,"[2] and thus another theme emerges in the rhetoric.

The plan of deliverance, as seen by the black rhetors, was not immoral, unjust, or ungodly but rather only the 'righteous strivings' of a persecuted people. Truth was used to sanction the hope of the oppressed. In this case, using the Old Testament text as a foundation, the preachers would proceed to the New Testament's "Ye shall know the truth, and the truth shall make you free."[3] Freedom was taken to mean much more than spiritual freedom, and often the audience only received the meaning that provided them with immediate reality—freedom from economic and social oppression. The truth was often no more than the preacher's latest interpretation of a passage or impression of the white race. Somehow the truth was to make the black masses free, and it is perhaps true to say that many were deceived when their preacher's vague truth effected little or no change in their oppressive situation. Even though the use of these concepts to galvanize the black masses failed to de-

[2]Proverbs 12:28.
[3]John 8:32.

liver them from their social degradation, it was an attempt on the part of the preachers to bring consolation.

Beyond and occasionally within the basic themes of justice, righteousness, and truth, the black preacher appropriated key expressions to his messages. Some of the common images used appear below:

'suffering children of Israel'
'written in God's Law'
'down in the valley of oppression'
'been to the mountain top'
'way down in Egypt's land'
'eternal ruin of devils'
'God will fight our battle'
'Let justice roll down like water'

Using these and other religious expressions, the black rhetors motivated the black masses to have hope, patience, and faith in the ultimate victory of right over wrong, of good over evil. Some saw the eventual downfall of a corrupt system as early as the first part of the nineteenth century. Although David Walker was not a preacher, his language shows a strong religious emphasis. In 1829 he wrote, "O Americans! Americans!! I call God—I call angels—I call men, to witness, that your *DESTRUCTION is at hand*, and will be speedily consummated unless you repent."[4]

The foregoing discussion considered the major religious themes of black rhetors. While these themes are still used in some quarters of the black community, they have been replaced by secular themes proclaimed by more militant rhetors.

William E. B. Du Bois, who was like a voice crying in the wilderness during his lifetime, has become the most productive source for the secular themes in the rhetoric of the black revolution. Throughout his career, Du Bois tried to appeal to the intellect of white America. He employed

---

[4]Herbert Aptheker, *One Continual Cry*, New York, Humanities Press, 1965, p. 108. All quotations from Walker's *Appeal* reprinted by permission of Humanities Press.

the themes of power, democracy, brotherhood, humanity, and justice. Unlike the justice of the religious images, Du Bois' justice was not a supra-rational concept signifying God's intervention in human history, but rather equal justice under the law. He spoke in concrete terms concerning the needs and aspirations of the black masses.

In recent years, power as a theme in the secular rhetoric of the black rhetors has superseded brotherhood. The emergence of Malcolm X as a charismatic spokesman for black nationalism is responsible for a new look at the American situation. Coinciding with the dethroning of religious solutions was the emphasis on secular answers to the black man's problems. In 1965, a black leader, speaking to a college group in Los Angeles said, "moral suasion has seldom changed the minds of those in power."[5] Probably echoing the sentiments expressed a thousand times in as many different ways by oppressed people, this black rhetor indicated the public shift from religious images to secular concepts. In the same year, Malcolm X's proclamation to "let the Klan know that we can do it [use violence] tit for tat"[6] was a further signal of the changing emphasis of the rhetoric to a more aggressive stance.

Yet it is only a reaction to the position of the white society. Consequently, as a recourse to evade the constant denial of full brotherhood by the society, the black rhetors suggest the possibility of seizing power for themselves. However, the black revolutionists have yet to articulate a plan for the organization and manipulation of power outside the white system.[7] Indeed, the black masses can only discover the strength of collective power within the total American society, because of their intimate history within this national

[5]Speech given by William Green to the Human Relations Club, Pepperdine College, Los Angeles, California, September, 1965.

[6]Malcolm X, *Malcolm X Speaks*, edited by George Breitman, New York, 1965, p. 113.

[7]The Nation of Islam is an obvious exception. Based on metaphysical and social concepts, the Black Muslim's separation policy is relatively well articulated. For an in-depth study of Black Muslims, see C. Eric Lincoln, *The Black Muslims in America*, Boston, 1961.

context. While power outside this frame of reference is not unthinkable, it is highly unlikely for some of the same reasons that the rhetoric of black separation soon exhausts itself.

Having witnessed the death of brotherhood through moral suasion as a rhetorical theme, the contemporary rhetor of black revolution suggests that morality might be encouraged by the wielding of power by blacks. According to the rhetoric of the black secular leaders, power allows the blacks to exhibit, in truth, a sense of worth. The reasoning behind this emphasis seems to be that no one can claim brotherhood with one who is not his equal. As long as the whites have economic, political, and military power exclusively, then it is impossible to consider the blacks equal; at most, they are the recipients of benevolent paternalism. In Malcolm X's manhood speeches, the intense interest in the black man helping himself and doing his own thing is a reason for a black writer to say of Malcolm X, "he was our manhood."[8] Following Malcolm X's lead, power as a major theme pervades the rhetoric of the black secular rhetors such as Stokely Carmichael, Maulana Karenga, H. Rap Brown, LeRoi Jones, and Huey P. Newton. Their belief, shared by some of the black preachers, is that the respect of the black man will come when he has something with which to bargain.

Although the use of the power theme in speeches and essays suggests an inward turn (the black man to his own potentials and abilities), the concept is militant to the extent that the acquisition of power always presupposes the relinquishing of power by another. If Karenga says "we will control South Central Los Angeles,"[9] he means that someone will have to give up control of that area.

In Chapter 1, we saw that the rhetoric of black militancy is aggressive. Inasmuch as the rhetors do not allow their

[8]See Malcolm X and Alex Haley, *The Autobiography of Malcolm X*, New York, 1964, p. 454. The expression cited was used by actor Ossie Davis at Malcolm X's funeral.

[9]Speech given by Maulana Karenga at Purdue University, December 12, 1968.

positions to be defensive, they refuse to be placed on the defensive when speaking of power. Utilizing the emotional reactions produced by the term black power, the black rhetor accomplishes terror without the accompanying physical violence. Unquestionably, however, the recent uprisings in the major cities of the nation do give those whites who are frightened by the terms a referent. While the referent is inadequate and perhaps distorted by looters and the holiday spirit, it nevertheless suggests to many white Americans the explosive potential within the society.

Even the names of various organizations in the black community emphasize power; for example, consider FIGHT, US, Black Panthers, Bootstrap, Afro-American Action Committee. Reflecting in their names the newness as well as the vitality of power as a concept, these organizations are peopled with blacks who consider the traditional civil rights groups such as Urban League, National Association for the Advancement of Colored People and even Congress of Racial Equality, to be archaic and conservative. Even though CORE's emphasis did change when Floyd McKissick embraced black power, it is still considered one of the old line groups by many black revolutionists.

In pursuing the concept of power, the black revolutionist uses other themes to establish his rhetorical aim. He is concerned with attacking the opposition and supporting his own position. Thus, the rhetor employs language that serves these dual purposes.

An analysis of the speeches and writings of the black secular rhetors reveals that there are four major recurring themes, insofar as prevalent topics are concerned. The black rhetors are convinced that all black people face a common enemy, that there is a conspiracy to violate black manhood, that America is a hypocritical country, and that unity among blacks must be achieved for liberation.

In research for this study, I heard and read speeches by many black militants, including Malcolm X, H. Rap Brown, Maulana Karenga, Bobby Seale, and Stokely Carmichael. The essential differences between these speakers were determined by temperament, intellectual vigor, stylistic expression, and manner of delivery, not by the basic content of their messages. Perceiving the same society, these black rhetors see similar obstacles to black liberation, and sanction almost identical action for the removal of those obstacles. Universally, the black militants see themselves as victims of the society, and agree with Malcolm X who said in his famous speech "The Ballot or the Bullet," "I do not speak as an American, but as a victim of this American system."[10]

Every speech I examined referred in some way or another to the common enemy. Some speakers used the term 'common enemy' within their speeches; others used such epithets as 'the man,' 'the white man,' 'Mr. Charlie,' and 'the one who's keeping you down.' The prevalence of this theme reminds one of how deeply imbedded in the black revolutionist's psyche is his anger. For in all things, the white man becomes the accursed symbol of corruption, race debasement, self-hatred, discrimination, white racism, and more than is admitted, the slavemaster. Just as the master was considered the enemy of the field Negro who had to be broken, so the common enemy today remains the same.

One method used by black organizers of rebellions and escape during slavery was to convince the reluctant blacks that 'we all got the same enemy.' Although it is true that some slaves had masters more sympathetic than others, the black organizers saw all slave-owners as the enemy. It is this vision that has come down to the militant blacks as they look on white America as the enemy bent on breaking the black man's will and spirit.

No aspect of black life is completely free of the enemy, according to the rhetors of black revolution. Malcolm X saw the common enemy in the ghetto shops, in the furniture stores, downtown, uptown, on the Southern plantations, and as employer in the factories. Calling for black self-help, Malcolm X declared, "any time you have to rely on your enemy for a job, you're in bad shape."[11] There is seldom

[10]Malcolm X, *Malcolm X Speaks*, edited by George Breitman, New York, 1965. p. 26.

[11]Malcolm X, "The Ballot or the Bullet," long playing record published by the Afro-American Broadcasting and Recording Company, Detroit, 1965.

any doubt in the minds of the audients of the black revolutionists about the referent for the enemy. Stokely Carmichael contends that "the man"[12] controls black neighborhoods, although he does not live in those neighborhoods. Black people have come to distrust the man who pervades their economic and political life. Using this basic distrust of white America, the rhetors of black revolution have shown the man to be the source and origin of the black man's fundamental problems in American society. In this way, it is clear that the man is used as an objectification technique for channeling the grievances of the black masses.

Another major theme expressed in the rhetoric of revolution is America's hypocrisy. The rhetor usually starts with the American Constitution as he demonstrates that the Constitution was not intended to include black people. Some rhetors, however, begin their arguments at the Declaration of Independence. They contend that the founding fathers had no intentions of bringing the blacks into the American society, and therefore the society was formed with a basic flaw, the inherent superiority of the white race. To correct this flaw, many black rhetors contend that the present system must be replaced.

The hypocrisy theme also is seen when the black rhetors accuse whites of holding American democracy up to the world as the most humanitarian government. While white America extols the virtues of Americanism, black people curse their American predicament. Malcolm X shouts to a black audience, "You and I haven't benefited from America's Democracy; we've only suffered from America's hypocrisy."[13] Carmichael draws thunderous applause when he indicts, "this country is too hypocritical."[14] He contends that if polarization of the races occurs, it is because the white Americans are too hypocritical to accept their "re-

<hr/>

[12]See Robert L. Scott and Wayne Brockriede, *The Rhetoric of Black Power*, New York, 1969, p. 87.
[13]Malcolm X, "The Ballot or the Bullet."
[14]See Charles Lomas, *The Agitator in American Society*, Englewood, New Jersey, 1968, p. 149.

sponsibility as the majority power to make the democratic process work."[15]

The black revolutionists have no illusions about America's willingness to eradicate its double standard in racial matters. They profess no faith in America's benevolent intentions toward black people in this nation, or any other nation. Indeed, the black rhetors of revolution believe that survival depends on the coöperation of all black peoples. They see the American Dream leading large American corporations to South Africa to partake in the exploitation of black labor; they see America's economic control of large portions of South America; and they know that this is a white man's government.

Eldridge Cleaver suggests in a speech that black people should follow Malcolm X's suggestion to involve the United Nations in the liberation of blacks in this country.[16] According to the black rhetors of revolution, if blacks had anything to do with the nation's policies then it would not be involved in Vietnam and in South Africa exploiting the colored peoples of the world. So the black revolutionist is certain that America is a hypocritical nation that bases its decisions on race. Some even give as proof America's political flirtations with Russia in an effort to link up white power against the colored peoples. The black revolutionists are saying that racism is America's basic hypocrisy, because it contradicts all of the myths handed down from the founding fathers.

Because of the racism ingrained in the American soul, black rhetors have often suggested that a new American Constitution should be written, one that would give the people a more favorable basis for developing a great society. Inasmuch as this rhetoric addresses the primary foundations of national origin, it is akin to the rhetoric of David Walker and William Lloyd Garrison, who called for a new compact of government. If the nation cannot deliver the rewards of

[15]*Ibid.*, p. 139.
[16]Eldridge Cleaver, "Political Struggle in America——1968," Peace and Freedom Party Forum, Oakland, California, February 11, 1968. This speech appears in Chapter 6 of this book.

democracy to all of its people on the basis of the present political contract, then blacks have reason to seek another solution.

In 1923, Marcus Garvey, convinced that America would never grant freedom and equality to black men, declared, "we are determined that we shall have a flag; we are determined that we shall have a government second to none in the world,"[17] as he encouraged blacks to join his back to Africa movement. In 1968, Professor Vincent Harding wrote that black power advocates shout, "Go to hell, you whited sepulchers, hypocrites. All you want is to cripple our will and prolong our agony. . . ."[18]

America's failure to deliver the fruits of democracy to the black masses has produced a colossal distrust of white America's intentions. Building on the reservoir of frustration that long years of dreams and promises deferred has created, the black revolutionists possess enormous rhetorical credibility. As Nathan Wright, Jr., puts it, "In all fairness, black Americans cannot be asked to make emotional commitments to white friendships into which white people have historically built a guarantee of soon or late frustration."[19] He continues that there is often a "black time-ingrained cynicism at the systematic way in which cards are stacked against black people."[20] In a recent essay, a black militant revealed that she came to understand that "there wasn't room enough in the society for the mass of black people, that the majority of Americans are acting in unbearably bad faith or in tragic ignorance when they project to their children the image of an American society where all men are free and equal."[21]

[17]Marcus Garvey, "Deceiving the People," in *The Black Power Revolt*, ed. Floyd B. Barbour (Boston: Porter Sargent, 1968), p. 57.

[18]Vincent Harding, "Black Power and the American Christ," in *The Black Power Revolt*, ed. Floyd B. Barbour (Boston: Porter Sargent, 1968) p. 91.

[19]Nathan Wright, Jr., "The Crisis Which Bred Black Power," in *The Black Power Revolt*, ed. Floyd B. Barbour (Boston: Porter Sargent, 1968) p. 117.

[20]*Ibid.*, p. 118.

[21]Jean Smith, "I Learned to Feel Black," in *The Black Power Revolt*, ed. Floyd B. Barbour (Boston: Porter Sargent, 1968) p. 209.

The more significant fact is that when the rhetors of black revolution speak of American hypocrisy, they are able to support their assertions with clearcut examples of the society's failure to deliver the promise. In fact, the black rhetors often know that many of their followers have never been visited by the American dream; they have only known "the American nightmare," as Malcolm X put it.[22] One cannot forget that Stokely Carmichael and H. Rap Brown were two of the leading black youths in the non-violent movement just a few years ago. Actually, they were engaged in teaching other civil rights workers the techniques of non-violent resistance; but the vision of black and white together was shattered too many times by the American society.

The distance between the American ideal and the black man's reality is the area of the black revolutionist's most effective grievances. Using the revealing dichotomies of America, the black rhetors rally their audiences. For example, the fact that blacks fight for democracy for the Vietnamese but are not granted full equality in America often is cited as proof of American hypocrisy. The black rhetors also point out that black children in America have a higher mortality rate than do Vietnamese children; that black soldiers from the South cannot even be buried in some city cemeteries; and that the Vietnamese could come to this country and receive greater acceptance than blacks. American hypocrisy then is used as an issue to influence blacks to seek redress by any means necessary.

Convinced that America will not make any significant efforts to correct the situation by vigorously attacking racism, the black revolutionist contends that his actions cannot be defined by the criminal who concocted black people's sufferings in the first place. Indeed, one tenet of the Black Panthers is that all black men held in Federal, state, county, and city prisons and jails should be released.[23] The Black Panthers contend that a racist system is responsible for the

[22]*Malcolm X Speaks*, p. 26.
[23]*The Black Panther*, January 25, 1969.

brothers being in prison because they are not tried by a jury of their peers.

Even though rhetoric employing the hypocrisy theme has been heard more vigorously lately, it has been around for many years. It also should be noted that there are still some blacks who believe that redress can occur within the present system even as they admit American hypocrisy. The black rhetor uses the black masses' unique position to know that the American pretense to humanitarian qualities is, in fact, only make-believe.

Somewhat related to the hypocrisy theme that pervades the black revolutionist's rhetoric is the conspiracy theme. The black rhetor attempts to demonstrate that America deliberately designs to deny the black man his full share in the society. Before the conspiracy theme is developed in some speeches, the rhetor cites many examples of hypocrisy, then he may cite instances where blacks had their homes invaded or were brutalized by the police or store keepers. Everything done by the white society is held in suspect by the black rhetors.

In a speech or an essay, the rhetor might encourage his audience to deal cautiously with, say, the Kerner Report,[24] because the man is not going to indict himself. In the rhetoric, the black revolutionist tries to convince his audience that they have no reason to trust the white man. Nathan Hare says, "I have no faith that—given the nature of its existing institutions, belief systems and practices—white America can fully rectify the situation."[25] Although this is not a statement suggesting a conspiracy, it does indicate the utter distrust many black rhetors have in America's

[24]Report of the National Advisory Commission on Civil Disorders. This report was a response to President Lyndon B. Johnson's executive order of July 29, 1967. A series of black uprisings that began in 1965 in Los Angeles, California, had spread quickly across the nation. The National Advisory Commission on Civil Disorders was headed by Otto Kerner, former governor of Illinois. The report was cited for its candor, as it placed the blame for black frustration on white racism.

[25]Nathan Hare, "How White Power Whitewashes Black Power," in The Black Power Revolt, ed. Floyd B. Barbour (Boston: Porter Sargent, 1968), p. 188.

present institutions; from this position, the conspiracy theme is easily drawn. Now we can understand the nature of a black revolutionist's rhetoric when he says, "the government is against you—that is, the White House, the Court and the Congress—they've got Negroes in a trick bag."[26]

Having no faith in the government, the black revolutionist is capable of contending that the government has a conspiracy against black people. Every action by the government becomes suspect in the black revolutionist's rhetoric. The white man is not to be trusted with anything or at any time because he "has fooled us too long and too much."[27] Examples of this monumental distrust can be found in almost any major American city where there is a planned parenthood organization in the ghetto. Black revolutionists claim that the centers are a part of the American conspiracy to eliminate the black people in this nation. They warn black mothers against taking the birth control pills because it will mean a reduction in the number of black babies born.

An argument often heard in support of the conspiracy theme is developed from the number of accidental and justifiable homicides committed in the black communities by the police. In 1966, the Progressive Labor Party came out with a broadside that purported to show "The Plot Against Black America."[28] It contended that under direct orders from Johnson and the White House racist cops and soldiers carried out vicious campaigns of terror against Black America. Throughout the essay, there are allusions to "well-planned" and "systematic" provocations on the part of the police. The killing of fifteen-year-old James Powell in New York by a policeman became identified with the police war against blacks in the rhetoric of the black revolutionists. Blacks in the ghetto are told by the black rhetors that

[26]Malcolm X, "The Ballot or the Bullet," long playing record published by the Afro-American Broadcasting and Recording Company, Detroit, 1965.

[27]Speech given by Maulana Karenga at Purdue University, December 12, 1968.

[28]The Plot Against Black America, New York, Harlem Progressive Labor Party, 1966.

every time a black person is killed by a policeman is simply the brutal expression of racism. This rhetoric is especially careful to mention that what the coroner's office rules as a justifiable homicide is nothing but cold murder.

Distrust in white America is also seen when the black rhetors tell their followers that white politicians are all playing a game to suppress blacks. The rhetors explain to their audiences that one white politician will say one thing and another will say something else, but in fact both are in agreement about black people. The technique of one man playing your friend while another poses as your enemy is called trickery by the black rhetors. Malcolm X suggested in a speech in Detroit that LBJ's best friend was Richard Russell, an arch racist.[29] He says in the speech that when LBJ deplaned after taking the oath of office for President, the first thing he wanted to know was "Where is Dickie?"[30] The speaker concluded that they must have been working in concert, if so, how could Johnson be the best friend of Russell's and the black man's friend at the same time? According to Malcolm X, they were in cahoots to deny the black man his liberation.

Even though most black revolutionists see some kind of conspiracy against America's black population, only a few have taken the extreme position that America plans to commit genocide. These few revolutionists insist that America is as racist and therefore as susceptible to genocide as Germany was during the Third Reich. Thus, they articulate their fears to their audiences in an effort to plant still more distrust of white America.

When one considers the daily examples of police overreaction in the black ghetto, the constant poverty of many black families, and the rabid prejudice that betrays many white Americans, it becomes clear how the rhetoric of black revolution can be made to appeal to the black community by the rhetor's skillful use of the conspiracy theme.

[29]Malcolm X, "The Ballot or the Bullet."
[30]*Ibid.*

A fourth theme permeating the rhetoric of black revolution is unity of the black community. It is something of a cliché with Black Power advocates to accuse 'the man' of trying to keep blacks from organizing. The rhetors tell their audiences that it has always been the strategy of the white man to divide and conquer. Seizing on historical examples of the white man's use of this strategy to overcome other peoples, the black revolutionist calls attention to the political unions that emerged in Africa after the intervention of colonial forces. Furthermore, the slavery experience is cited to give additional support to the contention that whites have used the technique of divide and conquer whenever they were faced with threatening situations. During slavery, the black revolutionist contends, the slaves from different tribes were placed together while slaves with the same culture background, heritage, and language were separated to keep them weak and powerless. The black revolutionist goes further to suggest that after slavery some blacks were made the Uncle Toms of the white man and were constantly running to the man with information from the black community. This situation occurred when the white man made certain 'Negroes' feel that they had an inside track to his ear, while others were not so fortunate. But the black revolutionist insists that the white man was using these house Negroes against one another.

Inasmuch as that was the white man's method of rule and control in the past, that will probably be his method for the future, the masses are told by the black revolutionist.

To avoid oppression, then, the black masses must get themselves together so that they can speak with one voice and move with one spirit. In 1968 at an organizational meeting of black faculty in California, Walter Bremond revealed that "the only way we can hope to obtain true freedom is through getting together. Even the black pimps are getting together now. They are organizing. You must organize."[31]

---

[31]Speech given by Walter Bremond at the University of Southern California, August, 1968.

In a speech at UCLA, Adam Clayton Powell argued that if other ethnic groups can have their organizations, then the blacks must have theirs.[32]

While there have been a number of traditional civil rights groups working in the black community, they have usually been shunned by the black revolutionists because of too much white control. Consequently, there has been a proliferation of black organizations in the last few years. Operating outside the influence of groups like the NAACP and the Urban League, these newly formed organizations seek to represent the lowest man on the totem pole. Preaching unity based on blackness, the black revolutionist apparently hopes to create a massive base from which to deal with the problems of black people in the American society.

Malcolm X was the great evangelist of black unity, especially as he saw it manifested in black nationalism. He argued that one could "stay right in his own church and believe in black nationalism."[33] Black nationalism was more essential to survival than the sect of a man's church, according to Malcolm X. In his famous retort to those who questioned the basis of his unity he said, "They don't hang you because you are a Baptist or a Methodist, they hang you because you're black."[34] In this statement, he defines the basis and the limits of black nationalism. In other words, these black rhetors say to the oppressed masses, 'take what you have and use it to your advantage.' Thus, the people are encouraged to rally around the one thing that keeps them down—their blackness. And in finding strength in their blackness, they become like the Jews who have been persecuted for their religion yet find much of their unity in their religious heritage. Once unity is accomplished, the rhetors of revolution contend that nothing will be denied the black people because of the significant power base that their unity commands.

[32]Speech given by Adam Clayton Powell at the University of California, Los Angeles, October, 1967.
[33]Malcolm X, "The Ballot or the Bullet."
[34]*Ibid.*

Unity, therefore, is a prevalent theme in the rhetoric of black revolution. Taken together with the themes of a common enemy, conspiracy, and a hypocritical nation, it becomes acceptable doctrine for the black masses who are eloquent proofs of so much of the rhetoric.

Suggested Readings

For materials on themes, attitudes, and ideas in the black community, see Malcolm X, *Malcolm X Speaks*, edited by George Breitman, New York, 1965; James Baldwin, *The Fire Next Time*, New York, 1962; John A. William, *This is My Country Too*, New York, 1965; Elijah Muhammad, *Message to the Black Man in America*, Chicago, 1965; Alex Haley, *The Autobiography of Malcolm X*, New York, 1965; Claude Brown, *Manchild in the Promised Land*, New York, 1965; and Nathan Hare, *The Black Anglo-Saxons*, New York, 1965. See also Eldridge Cleaver, *Soul on Ice*, New York, 1968, for a provocative discussion of the black man's frustrations.

4

Nature of the Black Audience

The rhetors of black revolution traditionally have had responsive audiences when speaking before churches, clubs, and mass gatherings. When their rhetoric has appealed to the members of the audience, they have received thunderous applause or other audible and visible signs of approval. The black audiences usually respond to the speaker in some overt manner, whether they approve or disapprove of the speaker's message. However, the response to an unfavorable message is more often silence and the response to a favorable message is usually vocal and visible signs. The degree and intensity of the generating response to the speaker largely depend on the speaker's reputation, style, and development of his ideas, as well as on his manner of delivery.

Black churches tend to have greater capacity for audible and visible response to a speaker than any other group of black listeners. This is probably the survival of the comfort and consolation syndrome prevalent in black plantation churches. In these churches, the listeners, moved by sin and guilt but much more by the need to release tensions brought on by the daily miseries of slavery, came forth with vocal responses to particularly consoling passages in the preacher's sermons. From a slight movement of the head in agreement with the speaker to a frenzied shout, visible response is manifest in many black churches by most adult listeners.

This almost universal response on the part of the audience plays a significant role in black rhetoric.

The speaker's original message is intensified by the listeners' sounding out their response. Often the black rhetor can judge his message on the basis of the audible and visible response of his audience. Many rhetors proclaim after a speech, 'Man, that talk really jelled,' or, 'They didn't seem to warm up to my speech.' It is clear in these statements that the black audience is considered by the rhetors to hold the key to effectiveness.

Inasmuch as the black rhetors attempt to gauge the audience's feedback in visible and audible expressions, they are aware of the significance of their audiences. Indeed, if an audience warms up to a speaker, he can get them to accept his ideas more readily and with greater ease. The usual audible response to a speaker in black churches is the fabled amen that punctuates the speech at regular or irregular intervals. Some speakers, especially talented black Baptists, can preach sermons with natural rhythms that allow the audience an opportunity to interject the amens.

Amen is not the only vocal expression from the black audience. Such interjections as 'Lord, help us,' 'that's right,' 'make your point,' and 'my Lord,' also indicate the audients' affirmation. At other times, the audience may take a key expression from the speaker's message and repeat it vocally. An instance occurred in a recent sermon when a popular black preacher said, "When I get near here, I need some one to pray with me."[1] The audience responded with, 'Pray with him,' 'Let's pray with him,' or 'We're praying with you.' Thus, in this situation, the speaker has a re-creative or expanding audience because the listeners reiterate and intensify the speaker's ideas in audible and visible responses.

Whether the preacher supporters (as the respondents are often called by other black churchgoers) actually listen

---

[1]Sermon by Dr. C. L. Franklin, New Bethel Baptist Church, Detroit, Michigan. Long playing record entitled "Job." Variations of this interaction can be heard on other of Dr. Franklin's albums including "Inner Conflict," "Jacob's Ladder," and "The Prodigal Son," all recorded by Chess Records. Dr. Franklin has cut over sixty albums of sermons.

to what is being said by the speaker has been debated by some black preachers as well as by laymen. Some contend that the respondents often do not understand or accept the speaker's message but rather are responding to the rhythm and cadence of the sermon or speech.[2] Although not universally true, there is some indication that this occurs. Some preachers have been known to get enthusiastic responses when quoting poets and philosophers with whom the audience would disagree if they understood the entire context of the quotation. In this case, the response of the audience conceivably is one of habit or respect for the speaker. Yet the generating force of the responsive audience is not negated by this suggestion; the interaction between speaker and audience is present even though its presence may only be habitual, or complimentary.

Responsiveness tends to become contagious in a highly emotional and dramatic situation. The speech situation often develops into a beckon and call occasion between the members of the audience and the speaker. In successful situations, the preacher is able to move the entire audience to total responsiveness. When this occurs, the listeners (who have now become overt participants) might weep, cry, or enter the extreme visible state referred to above as the shout. In churches where the shout is a regular part of the response pattern, there is usually one lead shouter (usually a female) who acts as a catalyst for other members of the audience. In fact, the shouter expresses her allegiance to the preacher's message by violent jerks of her limbs; her actions are often followed by other members of the congregation. An audience response that indicates active participation in the speech situation by audible or visible expression points to a generating audience. Thus, it is apparent by the preceding analysis that the black rhetors usually have re-creative audiences when they appeal to religious groups.

The response in the secular audience is less re-creative

---

[2]This view was expressed to the author on November, 1968, by Floyd Rose, a well-known preacher in Toledo, Ohio. Minister Rose preaches for the Ridgewood Church of Christ in Toledo, Ohio.

than the religious audience. Although the non-religious audience is not as vocal as the religious audience, the response patterns often parallel those of the religious groups. On a Harlem street in 1965, a black nationalist stood atop a wooden box to harangue a group of people on the conspiracy of the small merchants to oppress the community. As the speaker increased the tempo of his charges against the merchants, the audience began to interrupt with 'tell it like it is, brother,' 'speak the truth,' and 'yes.'[3] Making audible or visible expression of their acceptance and pleasure with the speaker's message, the listeners became a generating audience. Indeed, by supporting the speaker with favorable interruptions the audience heightens the meaning in the rhetorical situation for themselves.

Within most groups there are persons who favor and persons who oppose the position of the speaker. Affirmation of a rhetor's ideas by a sizeable proportion of an audience through vocal feedback helps persuade the uncommitted. The listeners who respond audibly become, in a sense, not passive receivers but active persuaders. However, the degree and kind of response is usually related to audience composition. The effect, then, on the uncommitted within an audience may well vary in relationship to how favorable the audience's composition is to the speaker. If the audience is composed of persons unresponsive to the speaker or his message, the persuasive influence will not occur as readily as when the audience becomes audibly and visibly responsive to the speaker. It is active affirmation within the black audiences that often helps to persuade the uncommitted.

In considering the kinds of response to a black rhetor, it is necessary to discuss some basic aspects of audience composition. There are three primary categories that can be examined in an effort to record the audience's reactions to the speaker's message: age, sex, and education. In black audiences, there are noticeable differences, depending upon

[3]The author made these notes in Harlem on August 16, 1965, while listening to an anonymous black nationalist speak on 125th Street, New York.

audience composition, on how listeners respond to a speaker's message. The following table suggests how black audiences respond according to age, sex, and education.

Audience Composition

Characteristics	Type of Audience
Age	
Adults	Religious
Youth	Secular
Sex	
Female	Religious
Male	Secular
Education	
Less	Religious
More	Secular

This table indicates the response patterns of black audiences according to three primary categories by demonstrating which groups would be more favorable toward a religious or a secular speaker. As shown in the table, there is a different emphasis between the adults and the youth.

For example, if the auditors are predominantly adults, their responses to the black rhetor will usually be audible and visible only when the message is religiously oriented. That is, the adult audience is more inclined to be involved in the interacting audience when the speaker is a preacher or when his theme is religious.

Few adults initiate audible reaction to a secular black rhetor. This is not to suggest that adults never engage in urging the secular black rhetors on in their speaking; actually adults compose a significant part of the black nationalist groups. Usually, however, the response to the speaker is more likely to be audible in a secular situation or when the speaker is not church-related if the audience is comprised of young people. Probably as a demonstration of the black youth's disenchantment with church-house religion, the small response patterns their parents engaged in within the church services are transferred, in part, to the secular world. Therefore, in an audience mainly consisting of young blacks, the rhetor is liable to find himself in a congregation of dispossessed worshippers whose response to the message is much like that of their forebears.

In much the same way as the difference of age relates to religious and secular situations, so does a difference in sex. The female auditors are more likely to be involved in the religious speech situation in an audible and visible manner, whereas the male listeners are more inclined to be similarly involved in the secular rhetorical situation. However, male listeners are among the chief supporters in the 'Amen corners' in many black churches. Yet women tend to be more totally involved in the visible and audible reactions in religious audiences. In many churches where vocal utterances and bodily actions indicate acceptance of the message, more than half of the respondents are women. Investigating the response patterns in twelve ghetto churches in South Central Los Angeles, I found that the women are more likely to respond audibly to the preacher's message than any other group of hearers with the exception of the 'amen corner' supporters. The small churches often do not have 'amen corners,' and in those churches women constitute the largest group of hearers and consequently the most vocal respondents.

The secular rhetor will discover a male audience more actively involved in his message than is a female audience. This does not mean that the black secular rhetor only finds response in a male audience, but rather that the men usually react to a non-religious speech more vocally than do women. It is as if the religious speech is an event for women, and the secular speech is intended for men. However, audiences are composites of people from various backgrounds and with different experiences and therefore seldom include only women or only men. In some cases, the secular audience (especially in instances of street corner speaking) will tend to be predominantly male. The speech situation rather than the speaker's theme is responsible for the low attendance of women in these cases. On the other hand, women usually comprise the larger number of attendants in church services in the black community.[4]

There is an observable difference between the less educated and more educated groups as regards response to religious and secular rhetors. From a survey made in some ghetto churches in Los Angeles, it was discovered that a significant proportion of those responding to the preacher with such audibles as 'Amen' and 'Thank God' were not high school graduates. In one congregation, nearly ninety-five percent of the preacher supporters did not have a high school education. The remaining five percent of the respondents constituted the church leadership.[5]

In secular meetings, the persons urging the rhetor on may come from all strata of society, but the more educated are less likely to react audibly in a religious meeting. Thus, Malcolm X, Maulana Karenga, Bobby Seale, Stokely Carmichael, and other militant black rhetors could evoke vocal affirmation from black college students much more readily than could a ghetto preacher. This circumstance is due to the listeners' suspicion of the rhetor. In fact, an audience of non-high school graduates would be skeptical of these speakers primarily because of the rhetorical symbolization employed by the rhetors. Conversely, educated listeners are inclined to affirm cautiously the language of the black preacher unless of course the preacher is considered to be together with himself, such as Ministers Franklin Florence of Rochester, New York, and Albert Cleage of Detroit, Michigan.

Whereas the less educated listeners have difficulty adjusting the strange outlook of black revolutionists to their Christian world view, interpreting Carmichael's secularism to their piety, or substituting Karenga's black nationalism for their 'white' religion, the more educated blacks find the

[4]The Black Muslim organization is an apparent exception to this rule. Because of the strong emphasis on male dominance in the family as well as in the mosque, Black Muslim services often have more men than women.

[5]Based on an unpublished preliminary study of the black pulpit by the author.

traditional black preachers less revealing of contemporary realities than are the black revolutionists. Thus, the response of both groups largely depends on their view of both the rhetor and his message. The less educated listeners are more willing to express themselves audibly in a religious setting, and the more educated respond audibly more readily to the secular situation. This might account for the more educated blacks attending churches where the audible or visible expression of agreement with the speaker is minimal, yet in an all black audience, these same people will readily express themselves.

Whether the self-expressionistic behavior of blacks in oral communicative situations is a product of the African heritage, of the early American evangelistic camp meetings, or of the slavery experience has not been established. But whatever the origins of this responsive phenomenon, the black revolutionists use it to their rhetorical advantage as the audience reiterates and re-creates the message. The short staccato sentences of the agitator are adapted to the response patterns of the audience. In a real sense, the audience and speaker often become engaged in concerted action with the speaker providing a signal, by which I mean an approving statement, and the audience providing the response indicating acceptance.

Suggested Readings

One of the first works done on the black church is William E. B. Du Bois, *The Negro Church*, Atlanta, 1903. For additional material, see Mark Fisher, *Negro Slave Songs in the United States*, Ithaca, New York, 1953. William E. B. Du Bois, *The Souls of Black Folk*, New York, 1961, is an interesting analysis of southern black culture, including religion and work. The section dealing with the Afro-American's music is especially good.

5

Origins of
Revolutionary
Themes

Many black rhetors have written and spoken passionately against the oppression of their people. Their appeals to the American conscience and to their people's hearts have sought the redress of grievances through traditional channels or by any means necessary. Using the small newspaper as an organ to disseminate their views, some of these black spokesmen were widely read and heralded by whites who sympathized with their cause. Others were impassioned orators who seldom spoke to large gatherings of whites but who often held hearers spellbound in small black social clubs, church conventions, and mass meetings for equality and freedom. It is unfortunate that many of these speakers, who embodied much of the oratorical genius of the black man, never wrote their speeches to be preserved for posterity. Unlike Booker T. Washington, who became a favorite of the white press and consequently the spokesman for the black man, these fierceless black rhetors responded to and molded attitudes and thoughts that now circulate in the black revolution. Among the men revered in the black community as spokesmen were J. C. Price; Kelly Miller; Reverdy Ransom; John Mercer Langston; George Washington Forbes; William H. H. Hart; Henry Highland Garnet; Archibald Grimke; Alexander Crummell; Roscoe Conkling Bruce; Samuel Ringo Ward; William Day; James Hayes; and Dean Pickens.

These men articulated the desires and interpreted the aspirations of many black men in the nineteenth and early twentieth centuries. They were the instruments that played out and on the emotions of an oppressed people, verbalizing the black man's quest for an elusive freedom. Convinced of the invincibility of the black race after so many years of slavery, discrimination, and physical abuse, these black rhetors spoke to the soul of the people.

Whereas some blacks had a message formulated to appeal to whites more than to blacks, the rhetors who spoke to black audiences were creators and carriers of concepts, beliefs, and ideas now expressed by the black militants. The authentic rhetoric of black America has always been militant and revolutionary. Sometimes the militancy was skillfully concealed if whites were in the audience, but the rhetor was always seeking to unify his followers for the eventual drive for total liberation.

Because whites have traditionally expected blacks to be less intelligent than themselves, they were seldom aware of the nuances of militant black rhetoric. This is one reason for the inability of whites to understand the overt aggressiveness of black rhetoric as expressed by many contemporary black revolutionists.

Blacks have been planning their liberation since the first slave was chained and sold on the auction block. And black speakers devised rhetorical subtleties to "deal with the man" that other blacks could understand.

An instance of the rhetorical subtlety that is meant to suggest militancy for blacks in an audience with a few whites occurred in a small rural church in the South. The preacher, observing that "the white gentleman in the audience is running for sheriff," continued his comments by saying, "we're happy to have him in our services because he might be the man we have to deal with one day." And as often happens with the black preacher, the speaker found a lesson in the word 'deal.' Thus, he said to his audience, "whenever you deal with anything, know what you are dealing with; some people never know what or who they are dealing with." Then he ended his statement about the visitor with, "Mr. Brown, we're gon' deal with you if you are elected sheriff and we're gon' deal with you if you never become sheriff." Even though it is difficult to convey in writing the actual speech situation, that is, the laughter in the speaker's voice during the speech and the facial expressions and the audience's affirmations of the speaker's words, this example is representative of the rhetorical underground resistance that blacks came to develop. The white politician left the audience confident that he had been able to win the support of the black preacher without much persuasion. Unknown to him, the black preacher had successfully articulated the feelings of his black audience.

At this point, it should be noted that if subtlety was a technique of the past, bluntness is the tactic of the present. The sign of the present black revolutionist rhetoric was the re-emergence of the candor and honesty with which David Walker blasted the American society in the early nineteenth century. During the 1830's, David Walker, a black Bostonian, shocked the white world by publishing one of the most powerful papers against human injustice America has ever seen. Almost every segment of American society condemned Walker's forthrightness in attacking the institution of slavery. Quakers even considered it to be a "bold, daring, inflammatory publication."[1] William Lloyd Garrison, serving as an assistant to the Quaker Benjamin Lundy, wrote that Walker's *Appeal to the Colored Citizens of the World* was "a most injudicious publication, yet warranted by the creed of an independent people."[2] On March 5, 1830, Garrison wrote "the circulation of this seditious pamphlet has proven one thing conclusively—that the boasted security of the slave states is mere affectation."[3]

The outrage of the white public against David Walker's pamphlet indicates the extent of its power. Walker not only indicted the society, but beyond that he also was audacious

---

[1] *The Genius of Emancipation*, April, 1830.
[2] *Ibid.*, February, 1830.
[3] *Ibid.*, March 5, 1830.

enough to address his paper to the 'colored citizens of the world,' which was an affront to many whites who considered the black man little more than an animal. The noted historian John Hope Franklin believes that the *Appeal* was "one of the most powerful antislavery tracts ever written."[4]

Coming prior to any major antislavery effort on the part of radical whites, Walker's *Appeal* was the catalyst for white sympathizers to join the call for emancipation. This idea runs contrary to the view held by some that benevolent whites sparked the anti-slavery movement. Black men were instrumental in agitating for their own freedom years before the largely white anti-slavery society began to function; and David Walker was one of the most courageous of the black agitators.

In answer to questions about the content and impact of Walker's pamphlet, the following discussion will cast light on both his appeals and his legacy to the black revolution. Much of the force of the *Appeal* is found in its uniqueness. David Walker was the first black man ever to write an indictment of Christian America that was circulated to many states. This in itself was a significant fact because of the white man's concept of what a black man should do and say. Walker demonstrated that black men feel, cry, get angry, and despise their oppressors as much as any other people. While it is true that much of the *Appeal's* effect occurred because no black man had ever written so violently against Christian America, it also is true that Walker's pamphlet appeared during a time of slave unrest and brought home to the American public the threat of physical violence on a large scale. This threat of tumult, riot, and rebellion in Walker's *Appeal* jarred white Americans. For the first time in American history, an African had decided to challenge religious America with the threat of physical violence from the slaves who toiled in the field and labored in the house. It was this situation that caused white Americans from diehard racists to Quakers to resist Walker's *Appeal*.

[4]John Hope Franklin, "Slaves Virtually Free in Ante-bellum North Carolina," *Journal of Negro History*, July, 1943, XXVIII, No. 3, p. 288.

Although Walker renounced, condemned, and berated Christianity, he did so by using Christian topics and themes. J. Saunders Redding writes:

> The *Appeal* was not directed to reason although there was reasonable matter in it: it was directed to the passions, in the name of God. Beneath the surface of religiosity unmeasured doses of poison gave off the odor of sulphur and brimstone.[5]

Indeed, Walker was calling down fire from heaven to consume the Christian Americans. Throughout the three editions of the *Appeal*, he invokes the Lord, God, and the angels to assist him in awakening America before doomsday.

The preamble to the *Appeal* contained the seeds of Walker's complete message. Twenty-nine times in the brief preamble he uses the term God or Lord, indicating his reliance on a basic Christian vocabulary. His repeated use of these terms shows his appeal to the Americans' belief in a just God. He opens the preamble by saying, the "coloured people of these United States are the most degraded, wretched, and abject set of beings that ever lived since the world began."[6] He intends to show that this condition exists because of maltreatment of blacks by an "enlightened and Christian nation."[7] Establishing a pattern for the essays that constitute the *Appeal*, Walker refers to America as a Christian nation four times in the preamble.

His initial strategy is to compare the treatment of the slaves in Egypt, Sparta, and Rome with those in America in order to demonstrate the cruelty of the American institution. Under a Christian nation, slaves were treated more wretchedly than in any pagan country, according to Walker. It appears to him that all the "wretchedness and endless miseries were reserved, apparently in a phial, to be poured

---

[5]J. Saunders Redding, *They Came in Chains: Americans from Africa*, Philadelphia, 1950, p. 90.

[6]Herbert Aptheker, *One Continual Cry*, New York, Humanities Press, 1965, p. 63. All quotations from Walker's *Appeal* reprinted by permission of Humanities Press.

[7]*Ibid.*

out upon our fathers, ourselves and our children, by *Christian* Americans!"[8]

He pleads that "God almighty, who is Father of our Lord Jesus Christ," open the hearts of Americans to "believe the truth."[9] On the surface, there is an evangelistic appeal to white America. In fact, the preamble contains many religious expressions and images, such as "suffering brethren," "appeal to Heaven," "God is just, as well as merciful," and "true hearted Christians and lovers of Jesus Christ."[10] These terms were apparently meant to appeal to the American sense of morality.

In discussing the plan for his articles, Walker calls attention to the source of the Africans' miseries in America. He believes that the "curse to nations"[11] that has spread terror and devastation among the blacks is slavery. While he indicates an awareness of the economic greed that motivated some "avaricious usurpers," Walker insists that Christian Americans must not forget that God rules in the armies of heaven and "among the inhabitants of the earth."[12] He sees God as arresting "the progress of the avaricious usurpers"[13] because slavery was the inhuman system from which most of the Africans' miseries originated.

Despite his indictment of' Christian America, Walker's view of the universe is biblical. He speaks of God as the Father and *"sole proprietor* or *master* of the Whole Human Family."[14] From this position, it is relatively simple for him to conclude that the Africans are in the family of God. Furthermore, if they are in God's family, then for God to be just he must treat all of his children equally. Intermittently, Walker reminds his readers that those who believe "God is a God of justice"[15] will accept the arguments in his

[8] *Ibid.*
[9] *Ibid.*
[10] *Ibid.*, pp. 63–68.
[11] *Ibid.*, p. 65.
[12] *Ibid.*
[13] *Ibid.*
[14] *Ibid.*, p. 67.
[15] *Ibid.*

pamphlet. He insists that the God of justice will not allow some to suffer without just retribution.

Using the Spaniards as examples, he points out that they cannot expect their destruction to be procrastinated while they are "oppressing the Lord's people."[16] And yet the Spaniards, "those avaricious wretches are calling for Peace!!!!"[17] Again he pleads with every man who has a heart to understand that God is a God of justice. Thus, he appeals to Americans to accept the fatherhood and fairness of God to motivate them toward the acceptance of brotherhood and dignity of the Africans. With this demonstration, he closes his "remarks on the suburbs, just to enter more fully into the interior of this system of cruelty and oppression."[18] How Walker deals with the interior of slavery system is set forth in his first article, called "Our Wretchedness in Consequence of Slavery."[19] He sets for himself two interdependent goals in this article: (1) to establish the sons of Africa as the most wretched, degraded, and abject set of beings that ever lived, and (2) to show the white Americans to be "more cruel than any heathen nation did any people whom it had reduced to our condition."[20] Proof of these two contentions is made on the basis of a historical survey of slave-holding societies. Walker begins by the Egyptians, Turks, Spartans, and Romans to get at the Americans. He sees the enslavement of the Jews by Egyptians as being more humane than that imposed on the Africans by the Americans. He begins this article by citing passages from the Old Testament on the slave conditions of Egypt. For example:

And Pharaoh, said unto Joseph, thou shalt be over my house, according unto thy word shall all of my people be ruled: Only in the throne will I be greater than thou.[21]

[16]*Ibid.*, p. 68.
[17]*Ibid.*
[18]*Ibid.*
[19]*Ibid.*, p. 69.
[20]*Ibid.*
[21]Genesis 41: 40.

Having cited the verse, Walker appeals to the American people, "not to show me a coloured President, a Governor, a Legislator, a Senator, a Mayor, or an Attorney at the Bar—But to show me a man of colour, who holds the low office of constable, or one who sits in a Juror Box, even on a case of one of his wretched brethren throughout this great Republic!!"[22] Walker decorates this essay with exclamation marks, hoping to dramatize the incongruity of the American way. For Walker, America was not a great republic, even though the American people considered it to be. His subtle disdain for white America is apparent when he contemplates the predicament of his black brethren. According to his argument, Egypt had allowed Joseph, a man from a different nation and race, to become a governor in the land, but nowhere in the United States has a black man been so much as exalted to a position as constable.[23]

He continues from Genesis 45: that Joseph received Asenath the daughter of Potipherah as wife.[24] In comparison to the above, Walker asks, "Do they not institute laws to prohibit us from marrying among the whites?"[25] Then he immediately explains that he "would not give a *pinch of snuff* to be married to any white person I ever saw in all the days of my life."[26] He further explains, "I only made this extract to show how much lower we are held, and how much more cruel we are treated by the Americans, than were the children of Jacob, by the Egyptians."[27] When he introduces the Egyptians in this argument, Walker emphasizes the fact that they were "such as we are—about the same as you see the coloured people of the United States at the present day."[28] His immediate intention is to compare Israel under "*heathen Pharaoh*" and the Africans under

[22]Aptheker, p. 70.
[23]*Ibid.*
[24]*Ibid.*
[25]*Ibid.*, p. 71.
[26]*Ibid.*
[27]*Ibid.*
[28]*Ibid.*, p. 70.

the "enlightened Christians of America."[29] Unlike the Egyptians, who allowed Joseph to intermarry, America makes laws to prohibit intermarriage, thus suggesting that Africans are sub-human.

Next, Walker cites Genesis 47:6, the verse in which Joseph is told by Pharaoh, "the land of Egypt is before thee: in the best of the land make thy father and brethren to dwell."[30] This passage is followed by the question, "Where is the most barren spot of land which they have given us?"[31] To dramatize the cruel plight of the African, Walker relates a story of a black man who labored night and day to purchase a house, and once he had moved his family into it "he was cheated out of his property by a white man, and driven out of the door!"[32] Thus, the Africans are considered to be under a more cruel oppressor than were the Jews in Egypt.

The final example of the Egyptians' less severe treatment of slaves is the acceptance by Pharaoh's daughter of Moses as a son. Walker indicts the Americans for the "insupportable insult" that the Africans were not of the human family.[33] To prove that white America is guilty of making this insult, Walker quotes from Thomas Jefferson's statement that blacks are inferior to whites. This thought evokes extreme passion from Walker as he invokes God to have pity. The religious invocations are followed by an appeal to black men against "our natural enemies."[34]

In this statement, we see a foreshadowing of one of the principal themes of the black nationalists of the twentieth century. They insist, as Walker did, that the white man must be considered a common enemy. Walker derides those Africans who would aid the enemy in keeping each other in "hellish chains of slavery."[35] He assures his readers

[29]Ibid., p. 71.
[30]Ibid.
[31]Ibid.
[32]Ibid., p. 72.
[33]Ibid.
[34]Ibid., p. 73.
[35]Ibid.

that the white Americans would not be able to drag "our mothers, our fathers, our wives, our children and ourselves around the world in chains and hand-cuffs as they do"[36] if they but unite and trust their secrets to each other. Walker counsels his readers not to strike the enemy "until you see your way clear."[37] In much the same way, Maulana Karenga says to his followers, "Don't ever show your stuff until you really mean to use it."[38] In a footnote to his statement, Walker explains that he does not mean "until God shall take us by the hair of our heads and drag us out of abject wretchedness and slavery."[39]

Although he does not call for armed insurrection in explicit terms, few blacks could misunderstand the implicit appeal of his language. He advises the blacks, "God has been pleased to give us two eyes, two hands, two feet, and some sense in our heads as well as they."[40] As a concluding thought to the idea of resistance, religion is made a part of Walker's appeal. He contends, "the man who would not fight under our Lord and Master Jesus Christ—ought to be kept with all of his children or family, in slavery, or in chains, to be butchered by his *cruel enemies*."[41]

Having analyzed his audience, he knew the emotional attachement many blacks had for religion; he therefore makes his appeal to their love for Christ. Skillfully, Walker connects insurrection with fighting for "our Lord and master Jesus Christ."[42] The man who would not fight for Christ in order to free his family and himself from slavery deserved no more than he received from his enemies, according to Walker.

The conclusion reached by Walker is that the Egyptians did not treat their slaves as cruelly as the Americans did.

[36]*Ibid.*
[37]*Ibid.*, p. 74.
[38]Speech given by Maulana Karenga at Purdue University, December 9, 1968.
[39]Aptheker, p. 74.
[40]*Ibid.*, p. 74, note.
[41]*Ibid.*, p. 75.
[42]*Ibid.*

And because the Africans were so degradingly mistreated, they had every right to resist the barbarity of their Christian enemies.

Walker's discussion of Egyptian slavery is his most detailed example, as revealed in an examination of the amount of space devoted to each slave-holding state. Indeed the Jews' enslavement theme had roots deep in American religion, and Walker took advantage of the familiarity of the subject. Before Walker, white American agitators had used the same symbolism to demonstrate their relationship to Britain. However, the utility of the symbolism was not the same for Walker in this article as it had been for the Americans during the period of revolutionary agitation. Yet the courageous black agitator sees the same relationship many of the colonists saw, that of oppressor and oppressed.

In continuing his argument, Walker next briefly compares the Turks to the Americans. He notes that a paragraph in a South Carolina paper read: " 'The Turks are the most barbarous people in the world—they treat the Greeks more like *brutes* than human beings.' "[43] In the same paper there appeared an ad that read: "Eight well built Virginia and Maryland *Negro fellows* and four *wenches* will positively be *sold* this day, to the highest bidder.' "[44] It astounds Walker, as it might any sensitive person, that the Americans had the audacity to speak of the barbarity of the Turks when in their own land, indeed reported in their own paper, were deeds almost unspeakably cruel. He can only conclude that the "Christian Americans" are the most cruel people in the world, and that the Africans are the most degraded.[45]

It is possible to catch a glimpse of the rhetoric that was to come in Walker's indictment of white America and in his attempt to make the African feel the common bond of oppression. The black militants of today believe that it is necessary to win the minds of black people who have been so dehumanized that life has little meaning. They attempt to

[43] *Ibid.*
[44] *Ibid.*
[45] *Ibid.*

do this in much the same way as Walker endeavored to move blacks to resistance by telling them how degraded they are in comparison to other people. It is common to hear black revolutionists speaking of the activity of the black, brown, and yellow people of the world. "The African and Asian people are gaining their independence, but you remain caught in the vise of oppression,"[46] and similar statements are heard at meetings of the black militants. Malcolm X was fond of saying, "The white man has fooled you into thinking that you are a second-class citizen, and in no other nation in the world is there such a thing as a second-class citizen. You're either a citizen or you're a slave."[47]

To establish further his contention that no nation has ever treated people as abjectly as the Americans did, Walker cites a case from ancient history. His opening sentence in this argument reveals his strong conviction that even in ancient history one could not find an example of inhumanity equal to that inflicted by the Americans upon the Africans. He writes, "The sufferings of the Helots among the Spartans, were somewhat severe, it is true, but to say that theirs, were as severe as ours among the Americans, I do most strenuously deny."[48] He asks for an example where the Spartans chained and hand-cuffed the Helots and dragged them from their wives and children, children from their parents, mothers from their suckling babes, wives from their husbands, "driving them from one end of the country to the other?"[49] He never allows his main point to escape him, as indicated when he reiterates, "The Spartans were heathens, who lived long before our Divine Master made his appearance in the flesh."[50] Walker's charges are devastating to the white Americans' idea of their humanitarianism and good-

---

[46]Malcolm X, "The Ballot or the Bullet," long playing record published by the Afro-American Broadcasting and Recording Company, Detroit, Michigan, 1965.
[47]*Ibid.*
[48]Aptheker, p. 75.
[49]*Ibid.*
[50]*Ibid.*

will. In a strategic move he asks, "O! Americans, I ask you, in the name of the Lord, can you deny these charges?"[51] He decries that the Americans have made provisions for the Greeks and Irish "who have never done the least thing for them," while the Africans have been inhumanly persecuted.[52]

Writing of slavery as it existed among the Romans, Walker says, "the world knows, that slavery as it existed among the Romans was, comparatively speaking, no more than a *cypher*, when compared with ours under the Americans."[53] In passing, he mentions that had Thomas Jefferson not written of the Roman slaves in one of his works, the comparison between the Roman and American slaves might never have appeared in the *Appeal*. Walker is confident, however, that the Roman slaves knew no circumstance as degrading as that experienced by Africans in America.

After acknowledging that whites had written rebuttals to Jefferson's severe remarks about Africans, Walker warns his black readers, "let no one of us suppose that the refutations which have been written by our white friends are enough—they are *whites*—we are *blacks*."[54] He thus indicates his belief that blacks must participate in their own defense before the council of reason. They could not allow the white man to speak for them. In this way, Walker anticipated the contemporary black rhetoric that calls for blacks to make their own defense by defining and explaining their own needs and actions. He also takes issue with Jefferson's statement that the Roman slaves were more cultured than Africans because "it is not their *condition* then, but *nature*, which has produced the distinction."[55] Walker exclaims, "See this, my brethren!! Do you believe that this assertion is swallowed by millions of the whites? Do you know that Mr. Jefferson was one of as great characters as ever lived

[51] *Ibid.*, p. 76.
[52] *Ibid.*
[53] *Ibid.*, p. 77.
[54] *Ibid.*
[55] *Ibid.*, p. 78.

among the whites?"[56] If Jefferson's idea of the African is so low, then what of the common white?

The rhetorical questions raised by Walker penetrate the very heart of the African's problem in America—white supremacy. Jefferson's conception of the African, like that of many whites, was of a sub-human who was by nature incapable of achievement. It was this falsehood that Walker struggled to dislodge. In a real sense, he was an amateur sociologist who understood the importance of conditions and circumstances on human development.

The Romans, according to Walker, permitted slaves to rise to positions of eminence in the state, but the Americans "instituted laws to hinder us from obtaining freedom."[57] Furthermore, he asserts that the Americans have made laws prohibiting black men from obtaining and holding office in the United States. If this be the case, Walker wants to know how can the blacks' condition be more lenient than that of slaves under the Romans?[58] Walker concludes this argument with six exclamation marks, indicating what he believes to be the impossible nature of the situation of the African who can not prove his abilities because of legal prohibitions yet who is constantly degraded for not showing those abilities.

Appealing more directly to his black readers to whom he smuggled many copies of the pamphlet, Walker asks: "Are we MEN!!—I ask you, O my brethren! Are we MEN?"[59] This question rings out like the assertion by some black militants to their audiences: "You are chumps! You are political chumps! No man can take what you have taken and not be called a political chump."[60]

These are for the rhetor's intent fighting words to stir the audience to action. Malcolm X was a skillful user of this technique when speaking before large black audiences.

[56]*Ibid.*
[57]*Ibid.*
[58]*Ibid.*, p. 79.
[59]*Ibid.*
[60]See Malcolm X, "The Ballot or the Bullet," long playing record published by the Afro-American Broadcasting and Recording Company, Detroit, Michigan, 1965.

He would outline for his audience what he considered manly traits and characteristics and then he would describe the actions taken by Negro leaders as being unworthy of men.

Walker hastens to answer his own inquiry by more pointed questions. "Did our Creator make us to be slaves to dust and ashes like ourselves? Are they not dying worms as well as we? Have they not to make their appearance before the tribunal of Heaven, to answer for the deeds done in the body, as well as we? Have we any other Master but Jesus Christ alone?"[61] The conclusion is obvious that no black man has an inferior status and no white man has a superior status before Jesus Christ. By his implicit answer, Walker has prepared his readers to respond to the question, "How we could be so *submissive* to a gang of men, whom we cannot tell whether they are *as good* as ourselves or not?"[62]

From this point forward, the argument centers on the whites' fitness to be master over blacks. In a railing denunciation, Walker declares, "the whites have always been an unjust, jealous, unmerciful, avaricious and bloodthirsty set of beings, always seeking after power and authority."[63] After this indicting passage, he says the whites in Gaul, Spain, and Britain have acted "more like devils than accountable men."[64] As history shows, this was not to be the last time that whites would be called devils.

By no means does Walker intend to allow the whites the comfort of claiming that they are Christians. In the next paragraph, he turns his attention from the Europeans as heathen to view them as Christians. His belief is that the whites are as cruel or more cruel than ever as Christians.

In fact, take them as a body, they are ten times more cruel, avaricious and unmerciful than ever they were; for while they were heathens, they were bad enough it is true, but it is positively a fact that they were not quite so audacious as to

[61]Aptheker, p. 79.
[62]*Ibid.*
[63]*Ibid.*
[64]*Ibid.*, p. 80.

go and take vessel loads of men, women and children, and
in cold blood, and through devilishness, throw them into the
sea, and murder them in all kinds of ways. While they were
heathens, they were too ignorant for such barbarity. But
being Christians, enlightened and sensible, they are completely prepared for such hellish cruelties.[65]

Walker's conclusion demonstrates his thesis: "the enlightened American Christians"[66] are the cruelest people
ever to live.

This article is the product of a black man deeply involved in his people's sufferings. In many passages, the
poetic passion emphasizes David Walker's tremendous concern for his black brothers who toiled in the American fields.
Perhaps motivated more by sympathy for the slaves than
hatred for the masters, Walker often found that his sympathy
and his hatred were interrelated. His writings reveal the
difficulty he had in reconciling the incongruity that existed
in America as a Christian nation.

This difficulty did not end with Walker's indictment of
America; but in his writing, one sees his own personal
struggle with Christianity. Indeed it appears that he had
been more thoroughly converted to the Christian religion
than many whites; this was the crux of his personal strivings
as he made sarcastic statements about enlightened Christians
and then called on the Christian's God for deliverance. The
alternating cycle of faith and despair may have been the
bitterness of a man tempted to eat rotten fruit. In the three
remaining articles of the *Appeal*, Walker concentrates on
the same theme—incongruities of enlightened and sensible
Christians. But throughout the articles, his desire for black
manhood stands at the center of his consciousness and
marks his rhetoric as significant for the black revolution.

When one has read David Walker's *Appeal to the
Coloured Citizens of the World*, one realizes Walker's legacy
to the black revolution. In fact, he anticipates the con-

[65]*Ibid.*
[66]*Ibid.*, p. 63.

temporary black power votarists in terms of style, rhetorical development, and viewpoint. However, Walker's religious symbolism and orientation are not as important in today's black power rhetoric as they were in his time.

As I have indicated, black militant rhetoric has more emphasis on secular than on religious themes.

Even without religious appellations and biblical symbols, contemporary black rhetoric possesses a resemblance to Walker's rhetoric in its directness. As Walker is poignant and unyielding, so are the black revolutionists. The language makes demands, satirizes, and vilifies. Furthermore, in his *Appeal* Walker attacks the slavery system and the American society fearlessly and candidly.

In the preamble to his essays, he entertains the possibility that he would be killed; but yet he was determined to protest. His protestations were not in uncertain terms. It might be objected that he was often irrational, but his unreasonableness was not so much a function of aimlessness as it was of disgust. Consequently, he attacks the system that gave rise to his frustration by violent railings. Contemporary black rhetors also are constantly engaging in verbal assaults rather than in defense of their positions. Their strategy is to show the opposition in the wrong and to heap on the charges. Thus, the black rhetors attempt to arouse the brothers by using sharp, cutting, invectives against the system they despise.

Walker's viewpoint suggests the reason for his aversion to the American system. He sees America as a Christian nation that has contradicted the spirit of the kingdom of God. This vision of the society affords him the opportunity to analyze the failures, criticize the practices, and deride the intentions of American Christianity. There exists for him only good and evil. The American system of slavery is unequivocally evil and reprehensible; on the other hand, the Africans must be considered good because they have never mistreated the white Christians. Indeed there is a certain *deja vu* in the outlook of the black power votarists. They see a similar dichotomy of good and evil, black and white—'Whitey is evil, but black is beautiful.' Experiencing the injustices and knowing the hardships of black men in his day, Walker loathed the American system and left a legacy of defiance.

David Walker was the first black man to disseminate his views to a large public by writing; Charles Lenox Remond was the first black man to appear regularly on the platform in protest against slavery. Remond was born in Salem, Massachusetts, February 1, 1810. His father, a native of the Caribbean island, Curaçao, arrived in America at an early age and took up hairdressing, a common occupation among free blacks in his day.

One year and four months after Charles Lenox was born, his father became a naturalized American citizen. Charles Lenox and his sister Sara were educated in the Salem, Massachusetts, public schools. When he was young, Charles Lenox showed a skillful use of language and often repeated the speeches of politicians he heard in Massachusetts. He later became actively engaged in using his oratorical talents for the liberation of his black brethren. As a black man, he was inescapably bound to the slave, though he himself was born free.

Charles Lenox Remond became an anti-slavery lecturer and influenced his sister to follow the same course, although she later became a physician. For several years, Remond headed the Essex County (Massachusetts) Anti-Slavery Society and was a prominent figure in state organization of the society. Because of his distinguished talents as a spokesman for the cause of slave liberation, the anti-slavery forces considered it wise to commission him as a lecturer against slavery on the circuit in various Northern states. In this capacity, Remond attained his most significant distinction as an orator. At the age of twenty-eight he toured Maine, Rhode Island, and Massachusetts with the anti-slavery organizer Ichabod Codding.

Remond was extremely impressive as an anti-slavery orator. Even though he did not possess the background of slavery experiences that was to characterize Frederick

Douglass, his successor on the anti-slavery platform, Remond possessed an unusual sincerity, which contributed to his personal appeal. As one of the seventeen members of the first anti-slavery society in America, Charles Lenox Remond possessed great ethical appeal in the cities he visited.

Before the rise of Douglass, Remond was the most famous black man in the country. Whenever the views of blacks were sought, people turned to Remond. One can speak of him as the first black leader in the same sense that Americans later came to know Booker T. Washington and Martin Luther King, Jr. Indication of Remond's fame and power is seen in the positions the white press took toward him. Remond was mentioned by both anti- and pro-slavery newspapers. The anti-slavery papers praised him as a fearless spokesman against the evils of slavery; the pro-slavery press considered him a threat to the slavery institution. Remond's speeches against the cruel treatment of the slaves by white Christian Americans were particularly threatening to the pro-slavery forces because Walker's *Appeal* and Nat Turner's rebellion were fresh in their minds.

Few orators have equaled the precise balancing of phrases and words exemplified in many of Remond's speeches. Gifted with the natural ability to turn a thought into a neat series or antithesis, Remond demonstrated remarkable stylistic prowess on the platform. Perhaps, however, he sometimes drew his art too clearly. Unlike Douglass, who was able to weave into the fabric of an address many complex but subtle stylistic devices, Remond's rhetorical devices appeared to stand out like glowing gems. Of course it is fair to say that whereas the reader of his speeches is aware of these devices, Remond's audiences may not have considered them distracting.

Coupled with the preciseness of his sentence structure was his skillful reliance on emotional appeal to sway his listeners. In fact, Remond was like a verbal puppeteer playing with the senses and minds of his audience. In the famous Hibernian Address to the Irish, delivered in 1841 before a reluctant but expectant audience, Remond demonstrated mastery of the rhetorical situation. In the process of speaking to the audience on the conditions of slavery, he occasionally used crude methods of complimenting his audience. Although these methods may have been obtrusive, they were never insulting. He reminded his audience that their land was "enlightened and intelligent" and that there were "many wise and good men" in Ireland who sympathized with the oppressed people of America.[67] He was careful to mention that his speech was about "liberty," the cause "dear to the Irish heart."[68]

Furthermore, Remond insisted that his audience not applaud too much; rather, he cautioned them to listen. In the middle of a sentence about Daniel O'Connell, the audience gives a thunderous cheer; Remond insisted that he wanted them to listen, at which point the listeners became quiet again. There is little doubt that Remond figured the mention of O'Connell would bring the Irish to their feet, but he hastened to complain that he had been off the subject when he commented about O'Connell.

Near the end of the address, he took his audience inside the degrading system of slavery to see a woman with a collar around her neck because she desired to visit her child in an adjoining house; he spoke of the branding of the word *slave* on men's arms and of the plight of two brothers whose father received honors for fighting in the American Revolution. The brothers had been captured and sold into slavery because they dared to visit Washington, D.C., for a funeral. After relating these incidents, Remond warned the hearers against making an emotional judgment. His pathetic appeal, quite like his stylistic attributes, must be considered coarse and pronounced; yet he succeeded in presenting an emotional picture of slavery that was sure to effect his listeners.

More than his boundless enthusiasm to tell the anti-

---

[67] All references to Remond's speech to the Irish are taken from the speech that appears in Chapter 6.
[68] *Ibid.*

slavery story to the world, Charles Lenox Remond's ideas for securing black liberation are his legacy to contemporary Afro-American rhetors. Remond saw America as a Christian nation incapable of overcoming the festering evil of slavery. To him, it was incumbent on the nation to redeem itself by dealing fairly with the slaves.

This belief led him to call for America's realization of the black man as a human being who should be dealt with on the bases of justice and fairplay. In some cases, he pleaded for America's acceptance of the blacks as brothers, citing from scriptures such as, "of one blood hath God made all the nations of the earth for to dwell."[69]

In his rhetorical development, he employed the same basic hope utilized by David Walker that was to become the hallmark of black orators, including Malcolm X. There is disillusionment about America in Remond's rhetoric. What was expected was not produced in the national character, and what was yielded was unexpected by the black masses. It seemed to Remond as it had appeared to Walker—that America was spiritually capable of delivering to the black man full participation in the society. Thus, both of these black rhetors constantly appealed to the Christian conscience of the nation's people, only to find that the nation was incapable of delivering to the black man full participation in society.

It appears that Remond, knowing the harshness of the slavery he described, would not immediately expect the American dream. As an orator, Remond had to deal with the essential contradictions in America. Indeed the shock effect is greatest when one least expects it. Had the black man never heard the rhetoric of the American Creed, had he never listened to the slavemasters' speeches on the value of liberty, had he never been forced into the churches and had he never heard Independence Day speeches about the glorious revolution, then, the meaning of his peculiar maltreatment, although not yet understandable, would have been considerably less contradictory.

[69] *Ibid.*

Further contributing to the contradiction that plagued Charles Remond was the American acceptance, however timidly, of the Christian tenets of love for brother and enemy. For black orators, and particularly for Charles Remond on the anti-slavery platform, it was absurd to think of America as Christian. But the Americans considered themselves Christian, and thus the origin of religious and ethical contradictions that helped to create black religion as opposed to white religion in this country.

To the present day, there is a difference between the religious thoughts of blacks and whites in America. This difference is manifest in the ecclesiastical rituals and ceremonies as well as in the actual philosophy of religion. The black man sees in white religion many contradictions that cannot be explained by whites because their religion has not questioned the differences. Thus we see the creation of a black religion that deals with the irony by becoming more particularized and sectarian than its white counterpart. The religion heavily emphasizes brotherhood, justice, love, and the dignity of man.

Since David Walker, most black rhetors have been aware of the inconsistencies in American life regarding the black man, even though not all of the rhetors have used these contradictions rhetorically. Remond used the religious image effectively when he appealed to "He who is the fountain of justice"[70] in order to show his own understanding of God. He suggested that justice must be granted equally to all men, not just to whites. He associated justice with the Christian God—a fact the white Americans either forgot or did not care to apply in their dealings with black men. In the Hibernian speech, after citing cases of cruelty against the black man, Remond exclaims, "If these things be the result of Christianity or of patriotism, may heaven deliver me from the influence of either!"[71]

Among black rhetors the inability of the American society to provide for blacks the same justice granted to

[70]Ibid.
[71]Ibid.

whites has been an exceedingly popular theme. This phenomenon is a result of blatant discrepancies that are vulnerable to the rhetor's purpose because white Americans appear unable to correct them. Many black rhetors are quick to identify John Newton as the gentleman who ran a slave ship and who later retired to write the Christian song "How Sweet the Name of Jesus Sounds" or to mention the Christian injunction "love your enemies" in the same sentence with the inhuman treatment of slaves or the systematic cruelty perpetrated against blacks since emancipation. From the list of avowed racists, the black rhetor is still able to find discrepancies between Christian teachings and practice in white America. These are obvious examples of what are perceived as contradictions by black rhetors.

The black masses have their own examples of this blatant duality in white America's standards. They have witnessed the truth of the black rhetor's message in their places of employment and in the merchandising marts. The most obvious examples are major American political figures. When the masses hear Governor Lester Maddox of Georgia say that God told him to make certain political decisions, they know that Maddox's religion is not their religion.

The gulf between theory and practice in America allows the black rhetor to attack a vulnerable part of the American society. For the blacks, American politics and religion have been both vulnerable and essential. They are vulnerable in the sense that neither the political nor the religious ideal has been practiced, and essential because without the religious and political ideals propagated by clergy and statesmen, the black rhetors might have been unable to speak. Indeed, the task of the black rhetors is to spark the nation to a more comfortable relationship between its theory and practice.

Remond saw this as a worthy aim and therefore vigorously attacked the heart of the problem by exposing the cruelties of slavery. During his lifetime, the essential dilemma of American society was no clearer than it was in white Christian America's treatment of the slaves.

Charles Lenox Remond's legacy to the contemporary black rhetors is his energetic participation in the first anti-slavery society, his unselfish devotion to his enslaved brothers, his unusual eloquence, and his rhetorical use of the theory-practice vulnerability pattern in American society.

With the increasing tempo of the anti-slavery campaign, other black voices were raised in protest against the cruelties inflicted on the Africans. Chief among the vocal protesters was Frederick Douglass. In the early 1840's, the eloquent former slave overshadowed the ailing Remond on the anti-slavery platform. His oratorical talents caused many of the leaders of the movement to urge him to travel on behalf of the society. Douglass was an ideal person to speak against slavery because unlike Remond he had been a slave and had undergone many injustices.

Frederick Douglass was born in Talbot County, Maryland, around 1817. His own knowledge of his mother was very scanty, as he reports in *My Bondage and My Freedom*.[72] Furthermore, he knew nothing of his father. To some extent, the absence of parental care was filled by a warm-hearted grandmother around whose plantation shanty the young Frederick's life centered.[73] When he was seven, his master, Aaron Anthony, who was also an overseer for Colonel Edward Lloyd, took the young boy to the Lloyd plantation, where Douglass ran errands and did simple chores. On this plantation, he experienced some of the harsher aspects of the slave's life, becoming familiar with unsympathetic attitudes, hunger, and cold.

In 1825, he was sent to Baltimore to live with a distant cousin of Aaron Anthony. For seven years, Douglass served as a houseboy in charge of Hugh Auld's son. At the death of Aaron Anthony, the young slave became the possession of Thomas Auld, who resided in St. Michaels, forty miles from Baltimore. Compared with the experiences that fol-

[72]See Frederick Douglass, *My Bondage and My Freedom*, New York, Arno Press and *The New York Times*, 1968, chapter one.
[73]This discussion of Frederick Douglass is based upon his own account as presented in *My Bondage and My Freedom*.

lowed the death of Anthony, the Baltimore sojourn was idyllic.

At his new home in the rural community of St. Michaels, Douglass showed signs of insubordination, which were later to be translated into actions. In 1834, his new master hired him out to Edward Covey, a professional slave-breaker, who was to provide the necessary conditioning. For six months, Douglass was flogged once a week, until he abruptly turned on Covey and gave him a thorough thrashing. The whip was abandoned for the four remaining months of hire. During the next two years, Douglass was hired out to a kind master, but he had reached the point in his aspiration for freedom where nothing else could satisfy him. He conceived a plan to escape to the North by paddling down the Chesapeake River to its head and then heading northward over land. But his scheme was prematurely revealed by one of the six conspirators who had planned to join him. Instead of putting Douglass into chains and selling him down the river to lower South plantation owners, his master, troubled by slavery, sent him back to Baltimore with a promise of freedom when he became twenty-five. For the next two years, he worked in the Baltimore ship-yards and persuaded Auld to allow him to bargain for his own employment in return for a weekly payment of three dollars.

His determination to go North was heightened in 1838 after a quarrel with Auld. Borrowing a sea-faring friend's identification paper with physical characteristics of the rightful owner on it, Douglass caught a train from Baltimore to Philadelphia. The train conductor deferred to a man in the naval service in the absence of the free papers that were required of all free blacks. On September 4, 1838, Frederick Douglass entered New York City to begin his indictment of slavery, which he called "the . . . foul, haggard, and damning scourge."[74]

In New York, Douglass was aided by David Ruggles, editor of the anti-slavery quarterly, *The Mirror of Liberty*,

[74]Frederick Douglass, *My Bondage and My Freedom*, New York, Arno Press and *The New York Times*, 1968, p. 430.

the first magazine edited by a black man. Ruggles also was secretary of the New York Vigilance Committee, which was formed to protect free blacks from being captured and sold into slavery and to aid escaped slaves. Ruggles sheltered Douglass in his editorial rooms. Twelve days after his escape, Douglass was married to Anna Murray, who had been born free in Caroline County, Maryland. After the ceremony, Ruggles gave Douglass five dollars and sent him to New Bedford, Massachusetts. In New Bedford, Mr. and Mrs. Nathan Johnson provided the Douglasses with board and lodging and the name by which history knows the eloquent opponent of slavery. His mother had named him Frederick Augustus Washington Bailey. But he dropped the two middle names and changed the surname to Johnson when he arrived in New York. The prevalence of the name Johnson among New Bedford blacks led his benefactor to give him the name Douglass.

Douglass' development as a significant spokesman against slavery began almost immediately after his arrival in Massachusetts. When he attended meetings of the New Bedford blacks, he was impressed with their platform talents and parliamentary abilities. In Baltimore, he had been a class leader in the Sharp Street Methodist Church, and in New Bedford he identified with the Zion Methodist Church, where his powers of self-expression sought religious themes. The New Bedford black community was a proving ground for Douglass' oratorical talents. But he did not allow the church to occupy all of his time; he discovered the anti-slavery society.

The fame of Frederick Douglass rests largely on his impassioned speeches that gave vent to his hostility toward slavery. Although many of his speeches contain numerous invectives, his oratory ranks among the highest in the annals of the English speaking world. His speeches indicate a mastery of the communicative situation comparable to that of Henry Grady, and a control of symmetry and dignity of expression reminiscent of Charles James Fox. Although Douglass' breadth of knowledge was unequal to Daniel

Webster's or Edmund Burke's, and although his forensic skills were not nearly as developed as those of the American and English masters, Douglass surpasses them both in the economy of his style. Because of his profound sincerity, which grew from personal experiences, he was able to speak without straining after effect. His words were easily produced because of the overwhelming truth to which he was witness. Frederick Douglass was his own argument and proof. Having on his body the scars of slavery's injustices, as he spoke he could dramatically bare the flesh for his audiences to see the imprint of barbarity.

His ideas were essentially less radical than many blacks believed them to be and yet more radical than the whites accepted them to be. He occupied the middle ground between the views held by men of his race. He was profoundly moved by the sufferings of the slaves, but he was not a revolutionist. He was actively engaged in indicting the slave masters, but he believed strongly in reform. This moderate view did not make him any less a proponent of what he called civil rights because he incessantly exposed the fallacies of the slavery argument, inveighed against American cruelty, denounced a Christianity that supported a slave state, recruited for the Union army, and would have fought himself had he been forced to. Yet, unlike David Walker before and many black rhetors after, Douglass never encouraged the slaves to revolt against slavery. He believed that the slaves could only be free if whites rejected the idea of slavery. Thus accepting the views and opinions of the Garrisonians, Douglass appealed to the moral conscience of white America.[75] Influenced by the speeches of Sheridan, Lord Chatham, and Fox, he read in the *Columbian Orator* and the association with Wiliam Lloyd Garrison, Charles

---

[75]There were several approaches to the emancipation of slaves. William Lloyd Garrison was the leading proponent of the appeal to the moral conscience of slave owners. Others, like David Walker and John Brown, believed in the use of violence to abolish slavery. For most of his life, Frederick Douglass was considered a Garrisonian. However, after 1851 he joined men such as Henry Highland Garnet and Samuel Ringgold Ward in favoring violence if necessary.

Remond, and Wendell Phillips; Frederick Douglass became one of the most powerful denunciators of oppression and vindicators of the rights of man in America. When Frederick Douglass died in 1895, Marcus Garvey was eight years old. Born in the small town of St. Ann's Bay on the Northern coast of Jamaica, Garvey was to become internationally known for his African nationalism. Never before had a black rhetor called for total separation from Western civilization with such persuasive appeal. Preparing for his life's mission, Garvey toured Costa Rica, Panama, Ecuador, Nicaragua, Honduras, Colombia, and Venezuela to observe the condition and status of the African laborers. In 1912, he journeyed to London in an effort to learn more about the circumstances of people of African descent in other parts of the British empire. His acquaintance with the African scholar Duse Mohammed Ali greatly stirred young Garvey's mind. He entered an English college for a few months and in his spare time read voluminously on the subject of Africa. Also in London Garvey read a copy of Booker T. Washington's *Up From Slavery*, which he later said sparked him to aspire to lead his race.

Now more concerned about the condition of black men than he had been earlier, Garvey went to Jamaica in the summer of 1914. On August 1, 1914, he established the Universal Negro Improvement and Conservation Association and African Communities League. Calling on all people of African parentage to join the movement to lift the race, Garvey explained that he intended to establish a central nation for the Negro race.[76]

Marcus Garvey landed in New York in March, 1916, to launch his international movement. The American blacks had been prepared by circumstances surrounding the end of the war as well as nearly sixty years of misery and discrimination for the acceptance of Marcus Garvey's radical proposals for African nationalism. Contrary to the belief of

[76]Edmund Cronon, *Black Moses*, Madison, Wisconsin, University of Wisconsin Press, 1968, p. 65.

one of Garvey's biographers,[77] the American blacks did not have to be prepared to accept a West Indian. Generally, blacks in the Western Hemisphere have always shared one another's sufferings. It was not uncommon in Garvey's day, nor is it uncommon now, to find West Indian blacks coöperating with and participating in American black organizations. What is strange is that his ideas found such rapid acceptance by blacks. But even this can be explained in terms of the black man's disillusionment with American society, which had failed to deliver to him the fruits of freedom. Discrimination against the black man, economic deprivation of the black family, and bigotry were still major factors with which the blacks had to cope. Garvey arrived, insisting that it was possible for a person of African parentage to escape this endless season of misery by joining his campaign to establish a homeland in Africa.

The outstanding themes in Garvey's rhetoric are pride and security. Garvey expounded his views of the proud African heritage of blacks. He often recalled the exploits of Zulu and Hottentot warriors against Europeans, histories of African empires, and slave rebellions led by Nat Turner, Denmark Vesey, and Gabriel Prosser. He delighted in pointing out that while Europeans were still savages, great civilizations flourished in Africa. Furthermore, he commanded his followers to teach their children that they were the descendants of African princes and kings. He believed that the black man needed to know his history and to feel pride at the mention of great heroes of black people.

Coupled with his stress on pride was often his insistence that black people be concerned about their own race more than any other. He warned the white man that no more African blood would be shed for him. "The first dying that is to be done by the black man in the future will be done to make himself free."[78] Garvey was active on many fronts to raise the black man's vision of himself. He successfully

[77]See Edmund Cronon's discussion of Garvey's adjustment to the tempo of American life in *Black Moses*, Madison, 1968, p. 38.

[78]Cronon, *Black Moses*, p. 66.

campaigned to get the news media to capitalize the word "Negro." Over and over again Garvey preached African nationalism to his followers, telling them that 400,000,000 black men awaited the liberation of Africa from the whites.

Thousands of American blacks were influenced by Garvey's movement. Malcolm X writes in his autobiography that his father became a field worker for the Garveyite movement in Michigan.[79] Other blacks who were not necessarily moved to actively campaign for Garvey did believe his rhetoric and were convinced that the establishment of race pride and security was essential to black dignity.

To demonstrate his message that blacks should own something, Garvey started several business ventures. His phenomenal success in New York had allowed him to purchase a large, six-thousand seat auditorium in Harlem. From this base, Garvey expanded his movement and started the Black Star Lines to travel between America and Africa. In addition, he set up the Negro Factories Corporation and the Universal Millinery Store. The Negro Factories Corporation was capitalized at one million dollars under a charter from the state of Delaware. Many black skeptics who had watched the spiraling growth of Garvey's movement from afar were convinced that he meant business in more ways than one. Garvey always placed strong emphasis on blacks owning their own businesses. While the rhetoric attracted many followers for the movement, the U. N. I. A., as the movement came to be called, never really had enough money to meet operating expenses for the far-flung ventures of Garvey.

Of significance to contemporary black rhetoric is Garvey's emphasis on black pride and self-respect. Many of the black leaders who denounced Marcus Garvey in his day later accepted his central philosophy: that for the black man to change his status, he needed to develop self-respect.[80]

[79]Malcolm X, *Autobiography of Malcolm X*, New York, Grove, 1966, p. 6.
[80]A. Philip Randolph, who proposed and organized a March on Washington in 1942, was one of the earlier critics of Garvey who saw

Even though it is true that the majority of blacks did not accept his return to Africa program, they were mesmerized by his broad knowledge of and love for Africa. It was as if they had found a leader who could voice their innermost sentiments and dreams without fear. His thunderous voice captivated the black masses when he spoke of the great African warriors and kings from whom they had descended. Although Garvey was not known for his strident denunciations of the white man, he was feared as a radical agitator who would disturb the peace. In 1927, he was deported from the United States, and although the U.N.I.A. continued to function for a while it never regained the momentum it had under Garvey's leadership in the early 1920's.

W. E. B. Du Bois, intellectual giant of the American black man, considered Marcus Garvey "either a lunatic or a traitor to his race."[81] There is no question that Du Bois' attacks on Garvey greatly affected the growth of the U.N.I.A. Garvey later blamed the failure of the movement on the criticism he received from the black intelligentsia and especially from Du Bois. In his later years, Du Bois appeared more sympathetic to the aims of the Garvey movement than he had been during his optimistic years. His criticism of Garvey even during the heyday of the U.N.I.A. was based upon the financial manipulations and erroneous assertions of the Garvey people. Du Bois was always the scholar seeking truth and honesty. He interpreted the Garvey movement as the brainchild of an organizational trickster who bilked the black masses out of hundreds of thousands of dollars. As a leader of the black intelligentsia, Du Bois felt that the 'talented tenth' of the black race in America could change conditions in this country without having to think of going to Africa.[82] What he saw in Marcus Garvey

---

value in his self respect philosophy. W. E. B. Du Bois, also a Garvey critic, later turned to Africa in his search for social peace. His decision to spend his last days in Ghana seemed to vindicate him from his earlier criticism of Garvey's back to Africa campaign.

[81]Cronon, *Black Moses*, p. 190.

[82]Harvey Wish ed., *The Negro Since Emancipation*, Englewood, Prentice-Hall, 1964, p. 73.

was not the 'talented tenth' but an example of a man not willing to prove himself in Western civilization. But in his old age, W. E. B. Du Bois went to live in Africa, where he could know the freedom and justice he had not known in America.

Du Bois' criticism of Garvey's movement is not his whole story. He was a fighter and crusader in his own right, although he never commanded the mass appeal of men like Garvey and Booker T. Washington. But while they could command large groups, Du Bois convinced and converted his disciples. For all of his popularity, Booker T. Washington never succeeded in persuading the black intellectuals that his program would bring black liberation. The primary obstacle to Washington's persuasive efforts was the counter-rhetoric of Du Bois.

Du Bois was thoroughly convinced of his own dignity and worth as a man. By the time he began in earnest to speak on the subjects of interest to the black man, he had competed with the white man in his academic communities, both in America and in Europe, and had demonstrated his ability. He was educated at Fisk University, Nashville, Tennessee, Harvard University, and The University of Berlin. Also because he was born in Great Barrington, Massachusetts, where he had been reared as an equal with the white children, he sought only full civil and political rights for the black man. Knowing the value of a liberal education, Du Bois insisted that the education of the black masses must be concerned with "the development of power and ideal."[83] He pressed for every single right "that belongs to a freeborn American, political, civil and social."[84] It is clear that Du Bois would have nothing to do with tokenism. He came almost to despise Booker T. Washington for asking for token gestures of goodwill. Du Bois contended that the black man was an American who had shared in the suffering,

---

[83]Herbert Aptheker, ed., *A Documentary History of the Negro People in the United States*, New York, Citadel Press, 1951, p. 907.
[84]*Ibid.*

building, and protection of the nation and as such should be given every privilege to which other Americans are entitled. He did not intend to procure favors of the white man, but rather proudly to demand rights.

He made no attempt to seek solutions to symptoms, but rather to strike at the heart of the matter. Not motivated by conciliation, Du Bois utilized the vocabulary of the warrior as he declared "The battle we wage is . . . a fight for ideals."[85]

The strategy of Du Bois was to indict and censure the hypocrisy of a nation that considered itself humanitarian. He could find little time for complimentary statements about a nation that grudgingly granted black men only tokens of their rights. Present day rhetors who are concerned with dignity, self-respect, and immediate full equality hold Du Bois in high esteem. His analytical mind looked beyond his own age to the time when America would have either revolutions or racial equality. He sought no stop-gap methods, no intermediate steps, but total freedom and liberation. Indeed, the great thinker's prophetic visions have their vintage in the rhetoric of black revolution.

It is apparent that when a political society grants some people participation while denying equal participation for other people, there will be protestations from the denied group. The spokesmen for the oppressed people may protest in different manners, but the rhetoric will tend to be aggressive. The witness of Floyd McKissick, Minister Franklin Florence, Stokely Carmichael, Reverend Albert Cleage, H. Rap Brown, Bobby Seale, Eldridge Cleaver, Walter Bremond, Malcolm X, Maulana Karenga, and others who seek to raise their people is directly akin to that of David Walker, Charles Remond, Frederick Douglass, Marcus Garvey and W. E. B. Du Bois. Whether their aim is reform or revolution, the contemporary black militants believe that America must make drastic changes in its political and social systems to guarantee equality and equity for blacks.

[85]*Ibid.*

Suggested Readings

For materials on black protest, see Francis L. Broderick and August Meier, *Negro Protest Thought in the Twentieth Century*, Indianapolis, 1965. This is a collection of statements and writings by a number of black leaders from Booker T. Washington to Malcolm X. Although this work covers the accommodation and Civil Rights periods thoroughly, it was published prior to much of the new militancy.

Additional information on protest may be found in W. Haywood Burns, *Voices of Negro Protest in America*, New York, Oxford, 1968; and JoAnne Grant, *Black Protest*, New York, 1968. Herbert Aptheker, *One Continual Cry*, New York, 1965, contains an excellent analysis of David Walker's incendiary pamphlet *An Appeal to the Colored Citizens of the World*. The best biography of Marcus Garvey is Edmund Cronon, *Black Moses*, Madison, 1968. See also William E. B. Du Bois, *Black Reconstruction*, New York, 1964; and Daniel C. Thompson, *The Negro Leadership Class*, Englewood, New Jersey, 1963.

6

Samples of Revolutionary Rhetoric

The history of the black man in America has been a series of protests. Proclamations of dignity, selfhood, equality, freedom, and justice have always been the black man's most personal confrontation with the speaking platform. The numbers and varieties of the spokesmen suggest the energy expended in the effort of black liberation. First, slavery was denounced; and after the emancipation, the black spokesmen turned their attention to the oppressive conditions brought on by segregation and discrimination. The black revolutionists voice concern over the presence in today's society of the same racist tendencies that have existed in the nation since 1619.

While they are aware of some change, they see the need for an even greater commitment on the part of the American society for liberty and justice for the black man. In this connection, it should be observed that the spokesmen labeled 'black revolutionists' in preceding pages are often only calling for drastic reform. There has never been a significant movement by blacks to overthrow the American government; to the contrary, blacks have sought to bring about more authentic changes in the American political, social, and economic system.

From the large number of speeches by black rhetors in the nineteenth and twentieth centuries, I have selected six speeches as examples of the rhetoric. Deliberately, I have avoided the speeches of such men as Booker T. Washington, Roy Wilkins, and Martin Luther King, Jr. Because they are not considered within the area of the rhetoric of black revolution, they are inappropriate subjects for this chapter.

The six speeches that appear in this chapter are: (1) Charles Lenox Remond's "Slavery and the Irish," delivered in Dublin, Ireland, in 1841; (2) Frederick Douglass' "Fourth of July Speech" delivered at Rochester, New York, July 5, 1852; (3) Adam Clayton Powell's "Can Any Good Thing Come Out of Nazareth?" delivered at the Howard University commencement exercises May 29, 1966; (4) Minister Franklin Florence's "The Meaning of Black Power," delivered in Kansas City, Kansas, September 10, 1967; (5) Eldridge Cleaver's "Political Struggle in America," delivered at the Peace and Freedom Party Forum in Oakland, California, February 11, 1968; and (6) Bobby Seale's "Free Huey," delivered at the Free Huey Rally in Oakland, California, February 17, 1968.

These speeches, which span more than one hundred and twenty-five years of protest, represent the progressive movement of the black revolution's rhetoric from the time of Charles Lenox Remond. Characterized by an aggressive stance against the *status quo* in terms of definitions, goals, and methods for black liberation, these speeches indicate the rhetoric's direction. In fact, one can readily see the shift from the elegant periods of Douglass to the language of the man on the street in Bobby Seale's speech.

This might be interpreted as the black man's attempt to discontinue talking the white man's language until blacks have united. However, one should not be misled to believe that there are no black militant spokesmen capable of speaking correct and proper English. Many of the most articulate theoreticians of the black movement are university professors and accomplished ministers. But insofar as they respond to the same sentiment as blacks in the central city concerning the need for black assertiveness, Eldridge Cleaver and Bobby Seale speak their language.

In providing a rubric for the reader, pertinent comment

on the speeches is needed. Remond's masterwork on slavery and the Irish swells with the optimism of a free-born man. Throughout the speech, one can sense his abiding faith in the spirit of man. Freedom, human nature, and holiness serve to light the fire of his heart as he speaks to the Irish audience. Reading Remond's speech, there is no reason to believe that he doubted the human spirit. America possessed the capability, spiritual and financial, to amend the critical slavery condition; and Remond's faith was that it would be soon if he could get the Irish to pressure America.

Douglass's *Fourth of July* speech is one of the great orations in American history. While Remond only dared to protest, Douglass dared to indict. Before his Irish audience, Remond was careful to demonstrate himself as a patriot. Before his American audience in Rochester, New York, Douglass praised from afar and admired only reluctantly. He could make rhetorical compromise that kept him firmly on the side of black radicals and white abolitionists. Had he praised America or the signers of the Declaration of Independence too much, he would have lost the support of many blacks. On the other hand, many of those who participated in the abolition movement also highly respected the signers of the Declaration. Douglass skillfully suggested that the point from which he had to view the signers of the Declaration of Independence was not the most favorable. His close association with John Brown, William Lloyd Garrison, and Wendell Phillips placed him in the radical tradition.

Over one hundred years after Douglass's speech, New York Congressman Adam Clayton Powell delivered his now famous black power speech in Washington, D.C., at the Howard University commencement on May 29, 1966. With more than thirty years of protestations behind him, Adam Clayton Powell has been called a "self-described Disciple of Protest."[1] During World War II, he published *Marching Blacks* and was consistently identified with civil actions on

[1]Claude Lewis, *Adam Clayton Powell*. Greenwich, Conn., Gold Medal Books, 1963, p. 5.

the part of Harlem residents. Thus, when he called for black power at Howard University, it was another step in Powell's long journey toward black liberation. A few days later, Stokely Carmichael led the chant for black power during a Mississippi civil rights march. Others participated in the chorus for black power, and before long, many movements were underway to find a single, simple, non-violent definition for black power.

The following year, the militant crusader for black rights, Minister Franklin Florence, revealed his definition of black power. Although this speech is not the most representative of his eloquence, it does present a realistic attempt on the part of a legitimate black leader to define black power. Indeed, after Stokely Carmichael's memorable chant around the bonfire in Mississippi, many leaders were having to provide definitions and explanations. The success of Minister Florence's struggle against Eastman Kodak Company and the launching of the manufacturing company FIGHTON with the coöperation of Xerox Company have made the dynamic preacher an influential spokesman in the black community.

Taking much of his rhetorical style from Malcolm X, Minister Florence believes in disciplined organization. Furthermore, in more than one speech he has praised Saul Alinsky, the community organizer, for teaching him the techniques of effective organization. Thus, Minister Florence's speech in Kansas City was a eulogy to the black community's ability to organize around the concept of black power.

Eldridge Cleaver, Minister of Information for the Black Panthers and accomplished essayist, demonstrates in his speech that many blacks have moved beyond the slogan black power to an acquisition of everything black as a rallying point. In other words, the reason of oppression has become the center for impassioned pride. Cleaver becomes an interpreter of the psychological ramifications of the Afro-Americans' acceptance of blackness as a positive concept. Thus, there is a clear movement from Florence's local organizational development of black power to Cleaver's universal doctrine of black togetherness. Cleaver is more the visionary who sees the significance of international black power as expressed in black awareness among African leaders and Afro-Americans. It also should be noted that Cleaver's interest in black awareness does not mean black exclusivity. He speaks of the need for radical whites to develop something to which blacks can relate so that a meaningful coalition can be formed.

Bobby Seale, Chairman of the Black Panthers, is what young blacks call a real soul brother. In his "Free Huey" speech delivered at a rally in Oakland, Seale speaks the language of the black masses. There is little attempt to dress his language in a form that will be acceptable to whites. Seale's respect for the highly venerated Huey Newton, Minister of Defense for the Black Panther Party, is told in the earthy grammar of the central city. In understanding the black community, Bobby Seale appears to know that he will communicate with his audience if he keeps to the language they best understand. In this speech, Seale handles the reality of black life as his audients know it in Oakland and makes of the occasion a communicating experience of one brother to another. Ultimately, this is what a true rhetoric must be.

These speeches represent only a small portion of the immense rhetoric of black revolution, but they indicate the intensity and contour that that rhetoric has taken in American history. To this collection could be added the speeches of Tommy Jaquette, Walter Bremond, Nathan Hare, Maulana Karenga, H. Rap Brown, and others; but this addition would only increase the quantity and not provide a significantly different quality than is demonstrated by the examples that follow.

Slavery and the Irish[2]

CHARLES LENOX REMOND

In rising to make some remarks on the great cause which has brought us together, I wish to preface them with one request: it is, that those by whom I am surrounded will do me the favor of listening to me as attentively and as noiselessly as they may—partly a consideration of my own health, and partly for their own sake. [Hear.] If I rise for one thing more than another, on the present occasion, it is to utter a few sentiments which are founded on the truth, and nothing but the truth, and such being the broad and immutable principle on which are grounded the doctrines I would propound, and the facts to which I would direct attention, I trust that you will not consider that anything which may fall from me is meant to be directed to any one sect or portion of the oppressed, but that my words are designed to have a general and unbounded application to all who suffer under persecution or sorrow, under the bondage of the enthraller. [Cheers.]

There is not a single individual, of all who surround me in this assembly, who may not have it in his power to promote and forward the glorious cause, to the advocacy of which I have devoted myself; nor is there one, the effect and benefit of whose exertions in behalf of the unhappy slave will not be felt and appreciated even in the remote land

2Reprinted from the *Liberator*, November 19, 1841.

from which I have traveled hither. It is not the lack of friends, nor of means, nor of publications devoted to our interests, which prevents our progressing as rapidly in this holy work as we would wish to progress; but I know from long experience that there is wanting, on the part of the people of Ireland, England, and Scotland, a strong and thorough conviction of the service and benefit which each individual man may, in his own person, render to the cause of liberty, by his own adhesion to our ranks. [Hear! hear!]

I mean not to deny that in your enlightened and intellectual land, my friends, there are many wise and good men who sympathize most cordially with us, and whose hearts bleed as they think of the heartless cruelty by which the slave is victimized; but keenly though they feel his wrongs, and deeply though they regret his sorrows, they are deterred from taking an active part in the efforts now making to restore him to the life of liberty, from the mistaken and most infatuated idea, that their assistance and coöperation could be but of little service. This is a fatal error, and one against which I cannot too emphatically forewarn you. [Hear! and cheers.]

It is the proud prerogative of all men—even of the most lowly and unobtrusive—to conduct in their own persons to the furtherance of the sacred cause of liberty and tolerance. Nor is it in words only that we should testify our love of freedom, and detestation of oppression. It is very easy to come here and pass resolutions laudatory of the one, and condemnatory of the other; but little advance will be made towards freedom's goal, by our resolving, unless we take care that the tone, tenor and practice of our lives shall keep pace with our professions. How fondly do I hope that all in this meeting—yea more, in this city, and even throughout the wide extent of your country—may be induced to regard the subject in this light, and to model the practice of their lives accordingly!

I stand here to advocate a cause which, above all others, should be, and ever has been, dear to the Irish heart—the cause of liberty. Nor do I pretend to ask from any

Irishman that which I would not always most willingly and delightfully concede to him, if the occasion should ever arise. [Loud cheers.] The request which I would make of you is the request of suffering humanity—the observations I would direct to you are the observations of justice and of truth; and, such being the case, surely there is no Irishman, worthy the name, who will consider that my request is unreasonable, or my observations ill-timed or out of place. The request which I now make, and have often made, is, that those who hear me will forget complexion, and that when the hateful truth is naked to their ears, that slavery exists in America, they will be inclined to consider the subject not as one of color, but of kind—not as one, the merits of which are to be decided by the hue of the skin, but rather one the test whereof should be the nature and character of the being who is enslaved. Enough! he is a man, and so are ye. [Cheers.]

Our love of freedom, our execration of tyrants and tyranny, are founded not merely upon our own individual principles, but also upon a grand and heavenly principle which we draw from the source whence all we have of noble and of good is derived—the source of holy writ. This is the principle which sways the mind of the society which I represent—such, too, I feel assured is the principle of the society I address; and while we can, with truth, make such an averment, there is not a slaveholder in America—there is not a slaveholder in Cuba—there is not a slaveholder in India, but must admit our principle to be good. They acknowledge that principle in their words, but act in defiance of it by their promotion of slavery. We, too, recognize the same heavenly principle, but be it ours to act in accordance with it, by loathing, contemning, and trampling under foot the unholy cause of bondage, meet it where we may.

Many there are, I grieve to say, who are deterred from the consideration of this subject through a vain and silly thought that the question is an elaborate and complicated one, and that in the discussion of it they would become bewildered and mentally blinded, as it were. 'Tis false, most corruptly false, to say so. There is no complication in the matter. The road lies before us, clear, straight, and un-warped as is the path of truth and justice. The question is resolved into two words only—liberty or slavery? And all men who acknowledge and reverence the one as pure and holy, and who loathe and execrate the other as hateful and infamous, ought to come forward and speak the sentiments of their hearts.

These are the few things I had intended to give utter-ance to as prefatory to the facts I will briefly lay before you in seconding the resolution commended to my charge—after which I will take occasion to make another motion in connexion with that brought forward by my friend Allen.

The question now before us—namely, that of slavery as it exists in the United States—is probably of greater moment and importance than that of the same evil as it may exist in any other land. This I say, not merely because there are in the United States a vast number of slaves, but also because I know that there are very many countries which, in this as in other respects, take their cue (so to use the word) from America; and of this I feel assured, that while the eyes of the whole world are directed to my own guilty country, the fingers of the wise and of the good in all lands are also pointed ignominiously at that glorious charter which she pretends to have adopted as the rule of her life, but which, day by day, desecrates and dishonors—therefore it is that I consider the behavior of America on the slavery question is looked upon with greater attention, and she exercises in this respect a more paramount influence by her example than does any other country. [Hear! hear!]

I know that in the pictures which I have drawn of the atrocities to which America is witness, and in the descrip-tions I have given of the horrors of the slave trade in that country, I am said to have been too severe and rather exaggerated. This, too, was said of the first man who ever mooted the question; but in my own case, as in his, my own breast tells me the charge is unfounded, and the accusation will only have the effect of making me more zealous and energetic in the vindication of truth and humanity. [Cheers.]

Some there are who are prevented from joining in the great struggle wherein we are engaged from a false and corrupt pride, for they consider (or feign to consider) that the vindication of the slaves' rights is an undignified employment; but I tell them it is an employment more dignified, more noble, more exalted than any other whatsoever in which man can be engaged. [Cheers.] It is not because the slave is a poor man, nor an ignorant man, nor a lowly man, that I profess myself his friend—it is because he is a despised man, an outraged man, a trampled man, a brutified man—one who, being a man as the best of you are men, is yet herded with the things that crawl and the beasts that grovel. [Loud cheers.] It is because I know that He who has promulgated to us all truth—who is Himself the fountain of justice—the source of truth—the perfection of loveliness—has announced from the hill of Sinai, that man cannot attempt the bondage of his fellowman without being guilty of a deadly crime. [Loud cheering.]

I mean not to draw an afflicting picture of the tortures to which the slave is subjected in the United States, and thus by harrowing your feeling, enlist your sympathies. Sufficient to say he is a man. You are yourselves of his nature, feelings, and character—in his sufferings you are tortured—in his indignities you are insulted. [Hear! hear! and cheers.] What care I how a man is murdered?—whether he be drowned, strangled, shot, stabbed, or beheaded, is to me indifferent. I only know that he is murdered, and it little boots to him or me whether the wretch be prostrated dead upon the plain in a moment of time—or whether he is murdered piecemeal in being condemned to a hateful, lingering existence, from which man would be relieved by death, and whereof the only solace is the hope of the grave. [Great applause.]

It has been said that for slavery as it exists in British India there is "Balm in Gilead," and it is with pleasure I assent to the proposition. [Hear! hear!] You have learned from my friend, Mr. Allen, how you in this country are situated with respect to British India. He has described to you in vivid and forcible language the position and capabilities of this latter country, and he has proved in the clearest manner how incalculable are the benefits which the people of Ireland, England, and Scotland have it in their power to confer not merely on those who suffer beneath the yoke of bondage in that fine colony, but even upon themselves, at home, by resolving on having recourse to the fertility of the British Indian soil, and the ingenuity of its population, for those tropical products which are now derived from other climes. [Hear! hear!]

Such, my friends, being the case, I ask you, are we looking for more than we ought to expect from the honor, virtue, and magnanimity of the British people, in expressing a strong and fervent hope that when they shall have considered the horrible nature and fatal tendency of slavery, they will unite as one man in adopting a measure which will at once promote their own interests, and exterminate that inhuman mode of traffic which pours forth human blood like mountain streams, and the continuing of which gives a death-stab to the high renown and glory of England? If you will not consent to do this, you avow yourselves part and parcel of that class of men who whirl the whip and bear the branding-iron. Ah! believe me, my friends, it is a noble work, that in which we are now engaged. [Hear! hear!] No reproaches of conscience—no inward chidings—no sighing after lost time can embitter the remembrance of this evening's proceedings; and I hope that, if the clock chimes ten ere we shall have concluded, there is none amongst us who will regret that we have devoted so much of our time to a noble task, the aim and object whereof is to raise the lowly, to exalt the afflicted, and strike the ignoble fetter from the dusky limbs of our fellowmen.

My bosom swells with pride and pleasure when I reflect that I am standing before Irishmen—men who in the year 1841 have the name of philanthropists. [Hear! hear!

and loud cheers.] Be it yours, my friends, to retain the lofty title, conditioned as you are as to your political influences, rather than having the name of republicans and democrats, to nurture slavery, and to countenance oppression. [Loud cheers.] Give me a monarchy—give me an oligarchy—give me an autocracy—yea, or even give me a despotic and tyrannical government, if, despite the pride of place and the "proud man's contumely," I see the living spirit of liberty blowing bright and imperishable in the people's breast, rather than a republicanism whose watchwords are, "Equality to all, and mastery to none," but whose deeds belie their splendid promises, and whose actions are those of oppression and persecution. [Cheers.] "Despotism" is a fearful scourge; but there is no delusion in the word. "Despotism" is not a sound which wins softly but deceptively on the ear, lulling it to ruin: it closes no man's mouth—it steals not away the sense—it blinds not the victim: stern and detestable in itself, it falls strongly and detestably on the ear; but give it to me, with all its horrors, rather than that which is in itself, a lie—professing, indeed, to be all that is sweet and goodly, but doing such deeds as, to think of, makes men's blood to freeze. [Immense applause.]

Flattering though this applause cannot but prove to my feelings, I will, however, experience a sentiment of far greater rapture, if, in some six or eight months hence, when in my own country, I shall learn that the call which I this evening make upon you has been responded to, not in words merely, but in deeds: then, indeed, will I feel great delight in having visited your Hibernian country; for I will know that I stood before men who have not merely professed their love and devotion for liberty, but whose life and actions are testimonials of the sincerity of the words they have uttered in witness thereof. [Cheers.]

One word more with reference to British India. It has been my high privilege, for the last few years, to have been associated with George Thompson, the eloquent advocate of the slave in the West Indies. He has been successful in his noble enterprise as regards the West Indies; and never

have I listened to him for half an hour upon this subject
that I did not feel the truth of what Mr. Allen avers, that if
Great Britain would strike the chains off the slaves in
America and elsewhere, it must be by giving encouragement
to India. In British India is to be found the instrument which
will put to death American slavery. If British India may produce, in as great excellence and abundance, those things
which are now imported from America at the expense of
slave toil, why should not Britain give the preference to
the former country? It is only consistent with her well-
known love of liberty that she should do so. Look to the
confessions of the slaveholders themselves, and you will
find it there avowed that the people of England, Ireland,
and Scotland, have this power vested in their own hands.
Many worthy persons in my own country are deterred from
giving their aid and coöperation to the antislavery cause,
from an apprehension which, to my mind, is exceedingly
silly and unfounded. [Hear!] Their objection to do so is, that
they imagine the slaveholders have, in their own hands, the
means of putting down all abolitionists, for that they (the
slaveholders) have threatened that, in case an effort were
made to emancipate the slaves they would dissolve the
American Union. Very many good and well-intentioned men
in America would have lent us their assistance long ago,
were it not for this threat, that the slaveholders would dissolve the American Union. Now, if in this assertion there
was or could be one iota of truth—the smallest particle of
rationality—I would grant that the objection should have
some weight; but the thing is preposterous; beyond all
parallel. [Hear! hear!] Why, the very thought is absurdity.
What does the American Union mean? Nothing more than
this, that the twenty-six States of America are joined together in government and civil rights. The Union is but a
parchment document, and as there is no hill so lofty that
it may not be surmounted, no space of ocean so boundless
that it may not be traversed, there is nothing more possible
than that the Union might be dissolved. But is it probable?
Suppose that the Union were dissolved tomorrow, by what

power or agency, let me ask, would it be possible for the holders to retain their slaves greater in number than themselves? [Loud cries of "hear! hear!"] To whom should the slaveholders look for sympathy, coöperation, and support, in their endeavors to keep these wretches in bondage? Will they look to the free States? Certainly not, for the very deed of dissolution precludes the possibility of that. Will they look to Mexico? No; for the Mexicans regard them with an eye of the rankest jealousy. Will they look to Canada? The thought is absurd. Will they look to the West Indies? What! ask men who are themselves but just liberated to aid in forging for other wretches! Who will believe it? Spain is the only land to which they can turn their eyes; but Spain has her own foes to trouble her, and the demon of slavery lurks within her own confines. Where, then, will they look for sympathy, and whither will they fly for aid? [Hear!] Every door is shut against them. Ah, Sir, believe me, the moment when the American Union is dissolved, that instant the power of the slaveholders is prostrated in the dust. Hopeless, helpless, friendless, they become an isolated class of beings, having nothing to depend on but their own strength, and that is weakness indeed. Then will rouse the crushed worm, turning on its torturer, and, in the fierce indignation of outraged men, the slaves will demand the right of measuring arms with their masters. [Immense cheering.] (A voice from the gallery—"Heaven speed the day!")

I do not think I shall myself live to see that day, but that such would be the effect of a dissolution of the American Union I feel confidently assured. [Hear!] Where is the man, who, if asked to become a slave, would not hurl back the offer indignantly in the teeth of the oppressor?—Nay, where is the woman—where is the child? The slaves of the United States are men, women, and children; and that they are as worthy this appellation, nay, worthier, perhaps, than the denizens of more favored lands, is amply testified by their patient and enduring conduct under contumely and outrage, for they, like yourselves, have preferred rather to suffer wrong than to do wrong. [Loud cheers.] I care not, then, for the insolent threat of those contumacious masters, for if the slaveholders of our country were to dissolve the Union sometime next year—if it were to be dissolved at twelve o'clock in the day, it is my firm conviction that before one o'clock (and that is but a single hour) there could not be found a solitary slave throughout the wide dominion of our land. [Cheers.] To suppose, therefore, that the slaveholders are serious in their haughty threat, bears absurdity on its very front: they'll never do it. They would not be so foolish—so thoroughly destitute of common sense as to dissolve the American Union, because forsooth it might be forbidden them to expose their slaves for sale, whip them with thongs, or brand them with iron within the confines of the land.

Is there amongst yourselves, think you, a single man who would be so detestably cruel, so utterly heartless, as to brand his sheep, his oxen, or his horse? For the sake of human nature, I trust there is not one; yet in the guilty land from which I have travelled hither, you will find men calling themselves republicans and patriots, who, with professions of universal equality ever in their mouths, and the words of liberty ever on their lips, can yet find in their hearts to stand unmoved and unaffected by, while the sleeve is turned up of the wretched helot's garment, and the noise of the red-hot iron, branding the word "slave" in the flesh of his fellowman is hissing in his ears (sensation). I ask of you are you men? and, being men, will you acknowledge or endure such a system as this? [No, no.] Who is there that can visit the Egyptian Hall in London, and having seen there the picture of a slave-market, will not turn away in disgust and indignation, and vow himself from that moment out the inveterate and implacable enemy of that atrocious system which brings ruin, infamy, and disgrace on human nature, and which can have first originated only in motives unearthly and infernal? Look at this state of things, and, freemen as you are yourselves, say will you suffer your fellowmen thus to be trampled on, and insulted with impunity?—Forget the past, but dwell with minds, calm as the intensity of your honest indignation will suffer them to be calm, on the present condition of the slave, and prove that you are worthy of the freedom you yourselves enjoy by aiding to unshackle him. [Loud applause.] Only picture to your mind's eye one man presuming in the face of high heaven, and before the civilized world to spread such wild havoc among his fellowmen as that which I have seen spread by a single slaveholder! When I see a woman condemned to wear such a collar as it were cruelty to bind around the neck of a dog, working in that collar, eating in it, aye, even sleeping in it, for no other crime than merely that of having asked permission to visit her child in an adjoining plantation—when, I repeat, I look on sights like these, my frame shudders with disgust—my blood freezes, and my heart bursts with indignation as I exclaim, "If these things be the result of Christianity or of patriotism, my heaven deliver me from the influence of either!" [Loud cheers.] Such is the system which prevails in many districts of the United States—such the hateful system that I beg of you to aid me in destroying. Who, sir, that looks around and views such scenes as have met my eye full often, could believe that we have the authority of heaven itself for averring, "that God has made of one blood the nations of men to dwell on all the face of the earth"? Yet, so it is. What I now demand of all Irishmen is, not merely that they should assent to the resolutions we may here propose, nor be content in merely promising that they will further my plans, but that their whole lives will be a system of unceasing warfare against the inhuman principles of slavery. And, in the name of truth and of justice—in the name of Him who is the God of truth and justice—in the name of dishonored humanity, and of the unhappy slave, whatever be the hue of the skin he wears, whether white or black, blue (if such might be) or red—I call upon you, Irishmen, to extend to the oppressed and enthralled man, under whatsoever sun he may be found, that aid and coöperation, that sympathy and affection, which you would wish, were you in similar circumstances, should be extended to yourselves. [Cheers.]

SLAVERY AND THE IRISH

I regret not, my friends, having made allusion to the brandings and other inhuman cruelties practised by the slaveholders on their unhappy victims—for, as soon will I believe the school-boy's wild and idle tale of the phantom who affrighted him, as believe that anything I have uttered can shock the delicacy of any around me. The recital will, I know, have a salutary effect upon the well organised mind. It may shock the sensibility, but it will inspirit you the rather to use your best exertions to annihilate this cruel system. I mean not here to be understood as saying that every slaveholder in America brands his slaves—I care not, though there be but one branded slave, it is enough for me. That one, so disfigured and disgraced, is a man, and it behoves not those, who are of the same kind, to stand quiescently by, and suffer such an outrage on their fellow-man. [Cheers.] Yet such an outrage is actually attempted under the American laws. Oh, let such laws be disowned and repudiated by all who love liberty and abhor oppression. Let Irishmen shun a land, however goodly, however fair, where deeds are done which call to heaven for vengeance—let them say to the Americans, "Long have we wished to visit your country; but never will we soil a foot by planting it on your shore until such enormities as now disfigure your national character shall have been done away with and atoned for."—[Cheers.] Let them tear the flag of freedom down, which flaunts absurdly over a recreant land which has nurtured oppression and makes liberty a mockery, while she pretends to extol its sacred cause.

When Mr. O'Connell—and now, that I have mentioned his name, let me take occasion to say how deeply I venerate that good and mighty man, who has put himself forth the undaunted and fearless champion of liberty and the rights of man in every clime the sun adorns. [A peal of applause here burst from the whole assembly which almost made the walls to shake, and which continued for several minutes.] I could wish, my friends, that if you consider me worthy the honor of your approbation, you would do me the favor of applauding with somewhat more of discretion and good judgment. I was about to say something with reference to a man who is justly dear to all your hearts, but you interrupted me in the middle of my sentence, and I am not sure that I have not forgotten all that I intended to utter. [Laughter and cheers.]

When, not many months ago, Mr. O'Connell, in the discharge of his duty as a public man and the advocate of liberty, asserted in his place in the House of Commons that there were to be found in Virginia many men who were not merely slaveholders, but even slave-breeders, and furthermore, that the gentleman who discharged the office of American ambassador at the English court, was himself a slaveholder, this latter person, instead of disproving the averment, challenged Mr. O'Connell to fight a duel. [Laughter.] As soon as he did so, and that the fact of his being a slaveholder had become known, that instant all Ireland should have raised her voice against him, and he should have been politely requested to pack up and return to his own estates, for that Irishmen were not in the habit of being called out to fight for having told the truth. [Cheers and laughter.] What a pretty fellow was this to represent a great nation at the court of St. James's!—a man who felt himself so troubled and scandalized by the truth, that the fighting of a duel was the only device he could have recourse to for healing his wounded honor. Such a man was not fit to have had a local habitation amid a free people. He ought to have been ashamed to have visited free and happy England. Can any more eloquent evidence be adduced of the state of things in my own guilty land than that which is comprised in this fact, that America despatches as her ambassador to the Court of St. James's, not the representative of human liberty—not a man whose life bore evidence of the zeal and faithfulness wherewith he obeyed the doctrines of republicanism, but a man who is himself actually one of the greatest slaveholders in the United States! Should the words which I now utter chance to reach the ears of Mr. Stevenson, it may be, perhaps, that he will challenge me, too, to fight a duel with him, but he should

wait until I had learned the art of doing so first, and I fear
that so long a postponement might be considered incon-
venient. [Laughter.]

But perhaps I am wandering from my subject. I hold
in my hand a resolution, which I will now read for you, and
for which I am anxious for your assenting voices. It is this—

"That we receive in the fullest acceptation the Scripture
declaration 'that God has made of one blood all nations of
men to dwell on all the face of the earth': and that to at-
tach any stamp of inferiority or degradation to any portion
of the human family, however the Creator has dyed their
skins of a deeper hue, is, in our deliberate opinion, at once
wicked and anti-Christian."

*   *   *

And now my friends, in resuming my seat, I have nothing further to say unless it be to express my unfeigned
gratitude, and that of the Antislavery Society, to the proprietor of this house, who, in the most generous manner,
has laid it gratuitously at our disposal. [Cheers.] It is a new
edifice, and if I were asked to what purpose a structure
intended for the service of the Irish public should on the
first night of its opening be devoted, I would unhesitatingly
say that the project which would most ennoble it and that
which would be dearest to the Irish heart, would be such an
one as we who are here assembled within these walls are
now engaged in—a project which derives its origin from
the best and purest feelings of our nature, and whose object
is none other than that holy and godlike one of elevating to
the station and glorious dignity of a man, him who is degraded and dishonored almost beyond the level of the
beast. If in the course of the remarks which I have this
evening offered, I may have said anything in reference to
my native country—America—which may perhaps be looked
upon as severe and unmitigated in its tone—I regret that I
cannot make amends—I grieve to think, not that I should
have so spoken, but that I should have been compelled so

to speak. [Hear! hear! and cheers.] I have testified only to that which I have seen—I have borne evidence solely to that which I have witnessed. With all her faults and all her follies, I cannot but regard my native land with feelings of the proudest affection, and I adopt with pleasure, as wholly consonant with my own sentiments, the beautiful lines of an American poet, once resident in England:

> I love thee—witness Heaven above
> That I, that land—that people love;
> And, rail thy slanders as they will,
> Columbia, I will love thee still.
> Nor love thee less when I do tell,
> Of crimes which in thy bosom dwell.
> Oh! that my weakest words might roll,
> Like Heaven's own thunder through thy soul.
> There is oppression in thy hand
> A sin corrupting all the land;
> There is within thy gates a pest,
> Gold and a Babylonish vest,
> Not hid in shame's concealing shade,
> But broad against the sun displayed.
> Repent thee, then, and quickly bring
> Forth from the camp the accursed thing;
> Consign it to remorseless fire,
> Watch till the latest sparks expire—
> Then, strew its ashes on the wind,
> Nor leave an atom wreck behind.
> Then shall thy wealth and power increase—
> Then shall thy people dwell in peace,
> On thee the Almighty's glory rest,
> And all on earth in thee be blest!

The Fourth of July[3]

FREDERICK DOUGLASS

Mr. President, Friends and Fellow Citizens:

He who could address this audience without a quailing sensation, has stronger nerves than I have. I do not remember ever to have appeared as a speaker before any assembly more shrinkingly, nor with greater distrust of my ability, than I do this day. A feeling has crept over me quite unfavorable to the exercise of my limited powers of speech. The task before me is one which requires much previous thought and study for its proper performance. I know that apologies of this sort are generally considered flat and unmeaning. I trust, however, that mine will not be so considered. Should I seem at ease, my appearance would much misrepresent me. The little experience I have had in addressing public meetings, in country school houses, avails me nothing on the present occasion.

The papers and placards say that I am to deliver a Fourth of July Oration. This certainly sounds large, and out of the common way, for me. It is true that I have often had the privilege to speak in this beautiful Hall, and to address

[3]Speech was delivered in Rochester, New York, July 5, 1852. It has appeared in numerous anthologies such as Carter G. Woodson, *Negro Orators and Their Orations*. Washington, D.C., Associated Publishers, Inc., 1925; Philip Foner, ed. *The Life and Writings of Frederick Douglass*. 4 vols., New York, International Publishers, 1950–55; and Roy L. Hill, ed. *The Rhetoric of Racial Revolt*. Denver, The Golden Bell Press, 1964.

many who now honor me with their presence. But neither their familiar faces, nor the perfect gage I think I have of Corinthian Hall seems to free me from embarrassment.

The fact is, ladies and gentlemen, the distance between this platform and the slave plantation, from which I escaped, is considerable—and the difficulties to be overcome in getting from the latter to the former are by no means slight. That I am here to-day is, to me, a matter of astonishment as well as of gratitude. You will not, therefore, be surprised, if in what I have to say I evince no elaborate preparation, nor grace my speech with any high sounding exordium. With little experience and with less learning, I have been able to throw my thoughts hastily and imperfectly together; and trusting to your patient and generous indulgence, I will proceed to lay them before you.

This, for the purpose of this celebration, is the Fourth of July. It is the birthday of your National Independence, and of your political freedom. This, to you, is what the Passover was to the emancipated people of God. It carries your minds back to the day, and to the act of your great deliverance; and to the signs, and to the wonders, associated with that act, and that day. This celebration also marks the beginning of another year of your national life; and reminds you that the Republic of America is now 76 years old. I am glad, fellow-citizens, that your nation is so young. Seventy-six years, though a good old age for a man, is but a mere speck in the life of a nation. Three score years and ten is the allotted time for individual men; but nations number their years by thousands. According to this fact, you are, even now, only in the beginning of your national career, still lingering in the period of childhood. I repeat, I am glad this is so. There is hope in the thought, and hope is much needed, under the dark clouds which lower above the horizon. The eye of the reformer is met with angry flashes, portending disastrous times; but his heart may well beat lighter at the thought that America is young, and that she is still in the impressible stage of her existence. May he not hope that high lessons of wisdom, of justice and of truth, will yet give direction to her destiny? Were the nation older, the patriot's heart might be sadder, and the reformer's brow heavier. Its future might be shrouded in gloom, and the hope of its prophets go out in sorrow. There is consolation in the thought that America is young. Great streams are not easily turned from channels, worn deep in the course of ages. They may sometimes rise in quiet and stately majesty, and inundate the land, refreshing and fertilizing the earth with their mysterious properties. They may also rise in wrath and fury, and bear away, on their angry waves, the accumulated wealth of years of toil and hardship. They, however, gradually flow back to the same old channel, and flow on as serenely as ever. But, while the river may not be turned aside, it may dry up, and leave nothing behind but the withered branch, and the unsightly rock, to howl in the abyss-sweeping wind, the sad tale of departed glory. As with rivers so with nations.

Fellow-citizens, I shall not presume to dwell at length on the associations that cluster about this day. The simple story of it is, that, 76 years ago, the people of this country were British subjects. The style and title of your "sovereign people" (in which you now glory) was not then born. You were under the British Crown. Your fathers esteemed the English Government as the home government; and England as the fatherland. This home government, you know, although a considerable distance from your home, did, in the exercise of its parental prerogatives, impose upon its colonial children, such restraints, burdens and limitations, as, in its mature judgment, it deemed wise, right and proper.

But your fathers, who had not adopted the fashionable idea of this day, of the infallibility of government, and the absolute character of its acts, presumed to differ from the home government in respect to the wisdom and the justice of some of those burdens and restraints. They went so far in their excitement as to pronounce the measures of government unjust, unreasonable, and oppressive, and altogether such as ought not to be quietly submitted to. I scarcely need say, fellow-citizens, that my opinion of those measures fully accords with that of your fathers. Such a declaration of agreement on my part would not be worth much to anybody. It would certainly prove nothing as to what part I might have taken had I lived during the great controversy of 1776. To say now that America was right, and England wrong, is exceedingly easy. Everybody can say it; the dastard, not less than the noble brave, can flippantly discant on the tyranny of England towards the American Colonies. It is fashionable to do so; but there was a time when, to pronounce against England, and in favor of the cause of the colonies, tried men's souls. They who did so were accounted in their day plotters of mischief, agitators and rebels, dangerous men. To side with the right against the wrong, with the weak against the strong, and with the oppressed against the oppressor! here lies the merit, and the one which, of all others, seems unfashionable in our day. The cause of liberty may be stabbed by the men who glory in the deeds of your fathers. But, to proceed.

Feeling themselves harshly and unjustly treated, by the home government, your fathers, like men of honesty, and men of spirit, earnestly sought redress. They petitioned and remonstrated; they did so in a decorous, respectful, and loyal manner. Their conduct was wholly unexceptionable. This, however, did not answer the purpose. They saw themselves treated with sovereign indifference, coldness and scorn. Yet they persevered. They were not the men to look back.

As the sheet anchor takes a firmer hold, when the ship is tossed by the storm, so did the cause of your fathers grow stronger as it breasted the chilling blasts of kingly displeasure. The greatest and best of British statesmen admitted its justice, and the loftiest eloquence of the British Senate came to its support. But, with that blindness which seems to be the unvarying characteristic of tyrants, since Pharaoh and his hosts were drowned in the Red Sea, the British Government persisted in the exactions complained of.

The madness of this course, we believe, is admitted now, even by England; but we fear the lesson is wholly lost on our present rulers.

Oppression makes a wise man mad. Your fathers were

wise men, and if they did not go mad, they became restive under this treatment. They felt themselves the victims of grievous wrongs, wholly incurable in their colonial capacity. With brave men there is always a remedy for oppression. Just here, the idea of a total separation of the colonies from the crown was born! It was a startling idea, much more so than we, at this distance of time, regard it. The timid and the prudent (as has been intimated) of that day were, of course, shocked and alarmed by it.

Such people lived then, had lived before, and will, probably, ever have a place on this planet; and their course, in respect to any great change (no matter how great the good to be attained, or the wrong to be redressed by it), may be calculated with as much precision as can be the course of the stars. They hate all changes, but silver, gold and copper change! Of this sort of change they are always strongly in favor.

These people were called Tories in the days of your fathers; and the appellation, probably, conveyed the same idea that is meant by a more modern, though a somewhat less euphonious term, which we often find in our papers, applied to some of our old politicians.

Their opposition to the then dangerous thought was earnest and powerful; but, amid all their terror and affrighted vociferations against it, the alarming and revolutionary idea moved on, and the country with it.

On the 2d of July, 1776, the old Continental Congress, to the dismay of the lovers of ease, and the worshippers of property, clothed that dreadful idea with all the authority of national sanction. They did so in the form of a resolution; and as we seldom hit upon resolutions, drawn up in our day, whose transparency is at all equal to this, it may refresh your minds and help my story if I read it.

> Resolved, That these united colonies are, and of right, ought to be free and Independent States; that they are absolved from all allegiance to the British Crown; and that all political connection between them and the State of Great Britain is, and ought to be, dissolved.

Citizens, your fathers made good that resolution. They succeeded; and today you reap the fruits of their success. The freedom gained is yours; and you, therefore, may properly celebrate this anniversary. The 4th of July is the first great fact in your nation's history—the very ringbolt in the chain of your yet undeveloped destiny.

Pride and patriotism, not less than gratitude, prompt you to celebrate and to hold it in perpetual remembrance. I have said that the Declaration of Independence is the *RINGBOLT* to the chain of your nation's destiny; so indeed, I regard it. The principles contained in that instrument are saving principles. Stand by those principles, be true to them on all occasions, in all places, against all foes, and at whatever cost.

From the round top of your ship of state, dark and threatening clouds may be seen. Heavy billows, like mountains in the distance, disclose to the leeward huge forms of flinty rocks! That bolt drawn, that chain broken, and all is lost. Cling to this day—cling to it, and to its principles, with the grasp of a storm-tossed mariner to a spar at midnight.

The coming into being of a nation, in any circumstances, is an interesting event. But, besides general considerations, there were peculiar circumstances which make the advent of this republic an event of special attractiveness.

The whole scene, as I look back to it, was simple, dignified and sublime. The population of the country, at the time, stood at the insignificant number of three millions. The country was poor in the munitions of war. The population was weak and scattered, and the country a wilderness unsubdued. There were then no means of concert and combination, such as exist now. Neither steam nor lightning had then been reduced to order and discipline. From the Potomac to the Delaware was a journey of many days. Under these, and innumerable other disadvantages, your fathers declared for liberty and independence and triumphed.

Fellow Citizens, I am not wanting in respect for the fathers of this republic. The signers of the Declaration of

Independence were brave men. They were great men, too great enough to give frame to a great age. It does not often happen to a nation to raise, at one time, such a number of truly great men. The point from which I am compelled to view them is not, certainly, the most favorable; and yet I cannot contemplate their great deeds with less than admiration. They were statesmen, patriots and heroes, and for the good they did, and the principles they contended for, I will unite with you to honor their memory.

They loved their country better than their own private interests; and, though this is not the highest form of human excellence, all will concede that it is a rare virtue, and that when it is exhibited it ought to command respect. He who will, intelligently, lay down his life for his country is a man whom it is not in human nature to despise. Your fathers staked their lives, their fortunes, and their sacred honor, on the cause of their country. In their admiration of liberty, they lost sight of all other interests.

They were peace men; but they preferred revolution to peaceful submission to bondage. They were quiet men; but they did not shrink from agitating against oppression. They showed forbearance; but that they knew its limits. They believed in order; but not in the order of tyranny. With them, nothing was "settled" that was not right. With them, justice, liberty and humanity were "final"; not slavery and oppression. You may well cherish the memory of such men. They were great in their day and generation. Their solid manhood stands out the more as we contrast it with these degenerate times.

How circumspect, exact and proportionate were all their movements! How unlike the politicians of an hour! Their statesmanship looked beyond the passing moment, and stretched away in strength into the distant future. They seized upon eternal principles, and set a glorious example in their defence. Mark them!

Fully appreciating the hardships to be encountered, firmly believing in the right of their cause, honorably inviting the scrutiny of an on-looking world, reverently ap-

pealing to heaven to attest their sincerity, soundly compre-
hending the solemn responsibility they were about to
assume, wisely measuring the terrible odds against them,
your fathers, the fathers of this republic, did, most deliberately, under the inspiration of a glorious patriotism, and
with a sublime faith in the great principles of justice and
freedom, lay deep, the corner-stone of the national super-
structure, which has risen and still rises in grandeur around
you.

Of this fundamental work, this day is the anniversary.
Our eyes are met with demonstrations of joyous enthusiasm.
Banners and pennants wave exultingly on the breeze. The
din of business, too, is hushed. Even mammon seems to
have quitted his grasp on this day. The ear-piercing fife and
the stirring drum unite their accents with the ascending
peal of a thousand church bells. Prayers are made, hymns
are sung, and sermons are preached in honor of this day;
while the quick martial tramp of a great and multitudinous
nation, echoed back by all the hills, valleys and mountains
of a vast continent, bespeak the occasion one of thrilling
and universal interest—a nation's jubilee.

Friends and citizens, I need not enter further into the
causes which led to this anniversary. Many of you understand them better than I do. You could instruct me in regard to them. That is a branch of knowledge in which you
feel, perhaps, a much deeper interest than your speaker.
The causes which led to the separation of the colonies from
the British crown have never lacked for a tongue. They have
all been taught in your common schools, narrated at your
firesides, unfolded from your pulpits, and thundered from
your legislative halls, and are as familiar to you as household
words. They form the staple of your national poetry and
eloquence.

I remember, also, that as people, Americans are remark-
ably familiar with all facts which make in their own favor.
This is esteemed by some as a national trait—perhaps a
national weakness. It is a fact, that whatever makes for
the wealth or for the reputation of Americans and can be

had cheap! will be found by Americans. I shall not be charged with slandering Americans if I say I think the American side of any question may be safely left in American hands.

I leave, therefore, the great deeds of your fathers to other gentlemen whose claim to have been regularly descended will be less likely to be disputed than mine!

My business, if I have any here to-day, is with the present. The accepted time with God and His cause is the ever-living now.

> Trust no future, however pleasant,
> Let the dead past bury its dead;
> Act, act in the living present,
> Heart within, and God overhead.

We have to do with the past only as we can make it useful to the present and to the future. To all inspiring motives, to noble deeds which can be gained from the past, we are welcome. But now is the time, the important time. Your fathers have lived, died, and have done their work, and have done much of it well. You live and must die, and you must do your work. You have no right to enjoy a child's share in the labor of your fathers, unless your children are to be blest by your labors. You have no right to wear out and waste the hard-earned fame of your fathers to cover your indolence. Sydney Smith tells us that men seldom eulogize the wisdom and virtues of their fathers, but to excuse some folly or wickedness of their own. This truth is not a doubtful one. There were illustrations of it near and remote, ancient and modern. It was fashionable, hundreds of years ago, for the children of Jacob to boast, we have "Abraham to our father," when they had long lost Abraham's faith and spirit. That people contented themselves under the shadow of Abraham's great name, while they repudiated the deeds which made his name great. Need I remind you that a similar thing is being done all over this country to-day? Need I tell you that the Jews are not the only people who

built the tombs of the prophets, and garnished the sepulchers of the righteous? Washington could not die till he had
broken the chains of his slaves. Yet his monument is built
up by the price of human blood, and the traders in the
bodies and souls of men shout—"We have Washington to
our father."—Alas! that it should be so; yet so it is.

> The evil that men do, lives after them,
> The good is oft interred with their bones.

Fellow-citizens, pardon me, allow me to ask, why am
I called upon to speak here to-day? What have I, or those
I represent, to do with your national independence? Are the
great principles of political freedom and of natural justice,
embodied in that Declaration of Independence, extended
to us? and am I, therefore, called upon to bring our humble
offering to the national altar, and to confess the benefits
and express devout gratitude for the blessings resulting from
your independence to us?

Would to God, both for your sakes and ours, that an
affirmative answer could be truthfully returned to these
questions! Then would my task be light, and my burden easy
and delightful. For who is there so cold, that a nation's
sympathy could not warm him? Who so obdurate and dead
to the claims of gratitude, that would not thankfully acknowledge such priceless benefits? Who so stolid and sel-
fish, that would not give his voice to swell the hallelujahs
of a nation's jubilee, when the chains of servitude had been
torn from his limbs? I am not that man. In a case like that,
the dumb might eloquently speak, and the "lame man leap
as an hart."

But such is not the state of the case. I say it with a sad
sense of the disparity between us. I am not included within
the pale of this glorious anniversary! Your high independence only reveals the immeasurable distance between us.
The blessings in which you, this day, rejoice, are not enjoyed in common. The rich inheritance of justice, liberty,
prosperity and independence, bequeathed by your fathers,

is shared by you, not by me. The sunlight that brought light and healing to you, has brought stripes and death to me. This Fourth July is yours, not mine. You may rejoice, I must mourn. To drag a man in fetters into the grand illuminated temple of liberty, and call upon him to join you in joyous anthems, were inhuman mockery and sacrilegious irony. Do you mean, citizens, to mock me, by asking me to speak to-day? If so, there is a parallel to your conduct. And let me warn you that it is dangerous to copy the example of a nation whose crimes, towering up to heaven, were thrown down by the breath of the Almighty, burying that nation in irrevocable ruin! I can to-day take up the plaintive lament of a peeled and woe-smitten people!

> By the rivers of Babylon, there we sat down. Yea! we wept when we remembered Zion. We hanged our harps upon the willows in the midst thereof. For there, they that carried us away captive, required of us a song; and they who wasted us required of us mirth, saying, Sing us one of the songs of Zion. How can we sing the Lord's song in a strange land? If I forget thee, O Jerusalem, let my right hand forget her cunning. If I do not remember thee, let my tongue cleave to the roof of my mouth.

Fellow-citizens, above your national, tumultuous joy, I hear the mournful wail of millions! whose chains, heavy and grievous yesterday, are, to-day, rendered more intolerable by the jubilee shouts that reach them. If I do forget, if I do not faithfully remember those bleeding children of sorrow this day, "may my right hand forget her cunning, and may my tongue cleave to the roof of my mouth!" To forget them, to pass lightly over their wrongs, and to chime in with the popular theme, would be treason most scandalous and shocking, and would make me a reproach before God and the world. My subject, then, fellow-citizens, is AMERICAN SLAVERY. I shall see this day and its popular characteristics from the slave's point of view. Standing there identified with the American bondman, making his wrongs mine, I do not hesitate to declare, with all my soul, that the character and conduct of this nation never looked blacker to me than on this 4th of July! Whether we turn to the declarations of the past, or to the professions of the present, the conduct of the nation seems equally hideous and revolting. America is false to the past, false to the present, and solemnly binds herself to be false to the future. Standing with God and the crushed and bleeding slave on this occasion, I will, in the name of humanity which is outraged, in the name of liberty which is fettered, in the name of the constitution and the Bible which are disregarded and trampled upon, dare to call in question and to denounce, with all the emphasis I can command, everything that serves to perpetuate slavery— the great sin and shame of America! "I will not equivocate; I will not excuse"; I will use the severest language I can command; and yet not one word shall escape me that any man, whose judgment is not blinded by prejudice, or who is not at heart a slaveholder, shall not confess to be right and just.

But I fancy I hear some one of my audience say, "It is just in this circumstance that you and your brother abolitionists fail to make a favorable impression on the public mind. Would you argue more, and denounce less; would you persuade more, and rebuke less; your cause would be much more likely to succeed." But, I submit, where all is plain there is nothing to be argued. What point in the anti-slavery creed would you have me argue? On what branch of the subject do the people of this country need light? Must I undertake to prove that the slave is a man? That point is conceded already. Nobody doubts it. The slaveholders themselves acknowledge it in the enactment of laws for their government. They acknowledge it when they punish disobedience on the part of the slave. There are seventy-two crimes in the State of Virginia which, if committeed by a black man (no matter how ignorant he be), subject him to the punishment of death; while only two of the same crimes will subject a white man to the like punishment. What is this but the acknowledgment that the slave is a moral, intellectual, and responsible being? The manhood of the slave is conceded. It is admitted in the fact that Southern statute books are covered with enactments forbidding, under severe fines and penalties, the teaching of the slave to read or to write. When you can point to any such laws in reference to the beasts of the field, then I may consent to argue the manhood of the slave. When the dogs in your streets, when the fowls of the air, when the cattle on your hills, when the fish of the sea, and the reptiles that crawl, shall be unable to distinguish the slave from a brute, then will I argue with you that the slave is a man!

For the present, it is enough to affirm the equal manhood of the Negro race. Is it not astonishing that, while we are ploughing, planting, and reaping, using all kinds of mechanical tools, erecting houses, constructing bridges, building ships, working in metals of brass, iron, copper, silver and gold; that, while we are reading, writing and ciphering, acting as clerks, merchants and secretaries, having among us lawyers, doctors, ministers, poets, authors, editors, orators and teachers; that, while we are engaged in all manner of enterprises common to other men, digging gold in California, capturing the whale in the Pacific, feeding sheep and cattle on the hill-side, living, moving, acting, thinking, planning, living in families as husbands, wives and children, and, above all, confessing and worshipping the Christian's God, and looking hopefully for life and immortality beyond the grave, we are called upon to prove that we are men!

Would you have me argue that man is entitled to liberty? that he is the rightful owner of his own body? You have already declared it. Must I argue the wrongfulness of slavery? Is that a question for Republicans? Is it to be settled by the rules of logic and argumentation, as a matter beset with great difficulty, involving a doubtful application of the principle of justice, hard to be understood? How should I look to-day, in the presence of Americans, dividing, and subdividing a discourse, to show that men have a natural right to freedom? speaking of it relatively and positively, negatively and affirmatively. To do so, would be to make myself ridiculous, and to offer an insult to your understanding. There is not a man beneath the canopy of heaven that does not know that slavery is wrong for him.

What, am I to argue that it is wrong to make men brutes, to rob them of their liberty, to work them without wages, to keep them ignorant of their relations to their fellow men, to beat them with sticks, to flay their flesh with the lash, to load their limbs with irons, to hunt them with dogs, to sell them at auction, to sunder their families, to knock out their teeth, to burn their flesh, to starve them into obedience and submission to their masters? Must I argue that a system thus marked with blood, and stained with pollution, is wrong? No! I will not. I have better employment for my time and strength than such arguments would imply.

What, then, remains to be argued? Is it that slavery is not divine; that God did not establish it; that our doctors of divinity are mistaken? There is blasphemy in the thought. That which is inhuman, cannot be divine! Who can reason on such a proposition? They that can, may; I cannot. The time for such argument is passed.

At a time like this, scorching irony, not convincing argument, is needed. O! had I the ability, and could I reach the nation's ear, I would, to-day, pour out a fiery stream of biting ridicule, blasting reproach, withering sarcasm, and stern rebuke. For it is not light that is needed, but fire; it is not the gentle shower, but thunder. We need the storm, the whirlwind, and the earthquake. The feeling of the nation must be quickened; the conscience of the nation must be roused; the propriety of the nation must be startled; the hypocrisy of the nation must be exposed; and its crimes against God and man must be proclaimed and denounced.

What, to the American slave, is your 4th of July? I answer; a day that reveals to him, more than all other days in the year, the gross injustice and cruelty to which he is the constant victim. To him, your celebration is a sham; your boasted liberty, an unholy license; your national greatness, swelling vanity; your sounds of rejoicing are empty and heartless; your denunciation of tyrants, brass fronted impudence; your shouts of liberty and equality, hollow mockery; your prayers and hymns, your sermons and thanksgivings, with all your religious parade and solemnity, are to Him, mere bombast, fraud, deception, impiety, and hypocrisy—a thin veil to cover up crimes which would disgrace a nation of savages. There is not a nation on the earth guilty of practices more shocking and bloody than are the people of the United States, at this very hour.

Go where you may, search where you will, roam through all the monarchies and despotisms of the Old World, travel through South America, search out every abuse, and when you have found the last, lay your facts by the side of the everyday practices of this nation, and you will say with me, that, for revolting barbarity and shameless hypocrisy, America reigns without a rival.

Take the American slave-trade, which we are told by the papers, is especially prosperous just now. Ex-Senator Benton tells us that the price of men was never higher than now. He mentions the fact to show that slavery is in no danger. This trade is one of the peculiarities of American institutions. It is carried on in all the large towns and cities in one-half of this confederacy; and millions are pocketed every year by dealers in this horrid traffic. In several states this trade is a chief source of wealth. It is called (in contradistinction to the foreign slave-trade) "the internal slave-trade." It is, probably, called so, too, in order to divert from it the horror with which the foreign slave-trade is contemplated. That trade has long since been denounced by this government as piracy. It has been denounced with burning words from the high places of the nation as an execrable traffic. To arrest it, to put an end to it, this nation keeps a squadron, at immense cost, on the coast of Africa. Everywhere, in this country, it is safe to speak of this foreign slave-trade as a most inhuman traffic, opposed alike to the laws of God and of man. The duty to extirpate and destroy it, is admitted even by our DOCTORS OF DIVINITY. In order to put an end to it, some of these last have consented that their colored brethren (nominally free) should leave this country, and establish themselves on the western coast of Africa! It is, however, a notable fact that, while so much execration is poured out by Americans upon all those engaged in the foreign slave-trade, the men engaged in the slave-trade between the states pass without condemnation, and their business is deemed honorable.

Behold the practical operation of this internal slave-trade, the American slave-trade, sustained by American politics and American religion. Here you will see men and women reared like swine for the market. You know what is a swine-drover? I will show you a man-drover. They inhabit all our Southern States. They perambulate the country, and crowd the highways of the nation, with droves of human stock. You will see one of these human flesh jobbers, armed with pistol, whip, and bowie-knife, driving a company of a hundred men, women, and children, from the Potomac to the slave market at New Orleans. These wretched people are to be sold singly, or in lots, to suit purchasers. They are food for the cottonfield and the deadly sugar-mill. Mark the sad procession, as it moves wearily along, and the inhuman wretch who drives them. Hear his savage yells and his blood-curdling oaths, as he hurries on his affrighted captives! There, see the old man with locks thinned and gray. Cast one glance, if you please, upon that young mother, whose shoulders are bare to the scorching sun, her briny tears falling on the brow of the babe in her arms. See, too, that girl of thirteen, weeping, yes! weeping, as she thinks of the mother from whom she has been torn! The drove moves tardily. Heat and sorrow have nearly consumed their strength; suddenly you hear a quick snap, like the discharge of a rifle; the fetters clank, and the chain rattles simultaneously; your ears are saluted with a scream, that seems to have torn its way to the centre of your soul! The crack you heard was the sound of the slave-whip; the scream you heard was from the woman you saw with the babe. Her speed had faltered under the weight of her child and her chains! that gash on her shoulder tells her to move on. Follow this drove to New Orleans. Attend the auction; see men examined like horses; see the forms of women rudely and brutally exposed to the shocking gaze of American slave-buyers. See this drove sold and separated forever; and never forget the deep, sad sobs that arose from that scattered multitude. Tell me, citizens, WHERE, under the sun, you can witness a spectacle more fiendish and shocking. Yet this is but a glance at the American slave-trade, as it exists, at this moment, in the ruling part of the United States.

I was born amid such sights and scenes. To me the American slave-trade is a terrible reality. When a child, my soul was often pierced with a sense of its horrors. I lived on Philpot Street, Fell's Point, Baltimore, and have watched from the wharves the slave ships in the Basin, anchored from the shore, with their cargoes of human flesh, waiting for favorable winds to waft them down the Chesapeake. There was, at that time, a grand slave mart kept at the head of Pratt Street, by Austin Woldfolk. His agents were sent into every town and county in Maryland, announcing their arrival, through the papers, and on flaming "hand-bills," headed CASH FOR NEGROES. These men were generally well dressed men, and very captivating in their manners; ever ready to drink, to treat, and to gamble. The fate of many a slave has depended upon the turn of a single card; and many a child has been snatched from the arms of its mother by bargains arranged in a state of brutal drunkenness.

The flesh-mongers gather up their victims by dozens, and drive them, chained, to the general depot at Baltimore. When a sufficient number has been collected here, a ship is chartered for the purpose of conveying the forlorn crew to Mobile, or to New Orleans. From the slave prison to the ship, they are usually driven in the darkness of night; for since the anti-slavery agitation, a certain caution is observed.

In the deep, still darkness of midnight, I have been aroused by the dead, heavy footsteps, and the piteous cries of the chained gangs that passed our door. The anguish of my boyish heart was intense; and I was often consoled, when speaking to my mistress in the morning, to hear her say that the custom was very wicked; that she hated to hear the rattle of the chains and the heart-rending cries. I was glad to find one who sympathized with me in my horror.

Fellow-citizens, this murderous traffic is, to-day, in active operation in this boasted republic. In the solitude of my spirit I see clouds of dust raised on the highways of the South; I see the bleeding footsteps; I hear the doleful wail of fettered humanity on the way to the slave-markets, where the victims are to be sold like horses, sheep, and swine, knocked off to the highest bidder. There I see the tenderest ties ruthlessly broken, to gratify the lust, caprice and rapacity of the buyers and sellers of men. My soul sickens at the sight.

> Is this the land your Fathers loved,
> The freedom which they toiled to win?
> Is this the earth whereon they moved?
> Are these the graves they slumber in?

But a still more inhuman, disgraceful, and scandalous state of things remains to be presented. By an act of the American Congress, not yet two years old, slavery has been nationalized in its most horrible and revolting form. By that act, Mason and Dixon's line has been obliterated; New York has become as Virginia; and the power to hold, hunt, and sell men, women and children, as slaves, remains no longer a mere state institution, but is now an institution of the whole United States. The power is co-extensive with the star-spangled banner, and American Christianity. Where these go, may also go the merciless slave-hunter. Where these are, man is not sacred. He is a bird for the sportsman's gun. By that most foul and fiendish of all human decrees, the liberty and person of every man are put in peril. Your broad republican domain is hunting ground for men. Not for thieves and robbers, enemies of society, merely, but for men guilty of no crime. Your law-makers have commanded all good citizens to engage in this hellish sport. Your Presi-

dent, your Secretary of State, your lords, nobles, and ec-
clesiastics enforce, as a duty you owe to your free and
glorious country, and to your God, that you do this accursed
thing. Not fewer than forty Americans have, within the
past two years, been hunted down and, without a moment's
warning, hurried away in chains, and consigned to slavery
and excruciating torture. Some of these have had wives and
children, dependent on them for bread; but of this, no account was made. The right of the hunter to his prey stands
superior to the right of marriage, and to all rights in this
republic, the rights of God included! For black men there
is neither law nor justice, humanity nor religion. The Fugitive Slave Law makes MERCY TO THEM A CRIME; and
bribes the judge who tries them. An American JUDGE GETS
TEN DOLLARS FOR EVERY VICTIM HE CONSIGNS to slavery, and five, when he fails to do so. The oath of any two
villains is sufficient, under this hell-black enactment, to send
the most pious and exemplary black man into the remorse-
less jaws of slavery! His own testimony is nothing. He can
bring no witnesses for himself. The minister of American
justice is bound by the law to hear but one side; and that
side is the side of the oppressor. Let this damning fact be
perpetually told. Let it be thundered around the world that
in tyrant-killing, king-hating, people-loving, democratic,
Christian America the seats of justice are filled with judges
who hold their offices under an open and palpable bribe,
and are bound, in deciding the case of a man's liberty, to
hear only his accusers!

In glaring violation of justice, in shameless disregard
of the forms of administering law, in cunning arrangement
to entrap the defenseless, and in diabolical intent this Fugitive Slave Law stands alone in the annals of tyrannical
legislation. I doubt if there be another nation on the globe
having the brass and the baseness to put such a law on the
statute-book. If any man in this assembly thinks differently
from me in this matter, and feels able to disprove my statements, I will gladly confront him at any suitable time and
place he may select.

I take this law to be one of the grossest infringements

of Christian Liberty, and, if the churches and ministers of our country were not stupidly blind, or most wickedly indifferent, they, too, would so regard it.

At the very moment that they are thanking God for the enjoyment of civil and religious liberty, and for the right to worship God according to the dictates of their own consciences, they are utterly silent in respect to a law which robs religion of its chief significance and makes it utterly worthless to a world lying in wickedness. Did this law concern the "mint, anise, and cummin"—abridge the right to sing psalms, to partake of the sacrament, or to engage in any of the ceremonies of religion, it would be smitten by the thunder of a thousand pulpits. A general shout would go up from the church demanding repeal, repeal, instant repeal!—And it would go hard with that politician who presumed to solicit the votes of the people without inscribing this motto on his banner. Further, if this demand were not complied with, another Scotland would be added to the history of religious liberty, and the stern old convenanters would be thrown into the shade. A John Knox would be seen at every church door and heard from every pulpit, and Fillmore would have no more quarter than was shown by Knox to the beautiful, but treacherous, Queen Mary of Scotland. The fact that the church of our country (with fractional exceptions) does not esteem "the Fugitive Slave Law" as a declaration of war against religious liberty, implies that that church regards religion simply as a form of worship, an empty ceremony, and not a vital principle, requiring active benevolence, justice, love, and good will towards man. It esteems sacrifice above mercy; psalm-singing above right doing; solemn meetings above practical righteousness. A worship that can be conducted by persons who refuse to give shelter to the houseless, to give bread to the hungry, clothing to the naked, and who enjoin obedience to a law forbidding these acts of mercy is a curse, not a blessing to mankind. The Bible addresses all such persons as "scribes, pharisees, hypocrites, who pay tithe of mint, anise, and cummin, and have omitted the weightier matters of the law, judgment, mercy, and faith."

But the church of this country is not only indifferent to the wrongs of the slave, it actually takes sides with the oppressors. It has made itself the bulwark of American slavery, and the shield of American slave-hunters. Many of its most eloquent Divines, who stand as the very lights of the church, have shamelessly given the sanction of religion and the Bible to the whole slave system. They have taught that man may, properly, be a slave; that the relation of master and slave is ordained of God; that to send back an escaped bondman to his master is clearly the duty of all the followers of the Lord Jesus Christ; and this horrible blasphemy is palmed off upon the world for Christianity.

For my part, I would say, welcome infidelity! welcome atheism! welcome anything! in preference to the gospel, as preached by those Divines! They convert the very name of religion into an engine of tyranny and barbarous cruelty, and serve to confirm more infidels, in this age, than all the infidel writings of Thomas Paine, Voltaire, and Bolingbroke put together have done! These ministers make religion a cold and flinty-hearted thing, having neither principles of right action nor bowels of compassion. They strip the love of God of its beauty and leave the throne of religion a huge, horrible, repulsive form. It is a religion for oppressors, tyrants, man-stealers, and thugs. It is not that "pure and undefiled religion" which is from above, and which is "first pure, then peaceable, easy to be entreated, full of mercy and good fruits, without partiality, and without hypocrisy." But a religion which favors the rich against the poor; which exalts the proud above the humble; which divides mankind into two classes, tyrants and slaves; which says to the man in chains, stay there; and to the oppressor, oppress on; it is a religion which may be professed and enjoyed by all the robbers and enslavers of mankind; it makes God a respecter of persons, denies his fatherhood of the race, and tramples in the dust the great truth of the brotherhood of man. All this we affirm to be true of the popular church, and the popular worship of our land and nation—a religion, a church, and a worship which, on the authority of inspired wisdom, we pronounce to be an abomination in the sight of God. In the language of Isaiah, the American church might be well addressed,

> Bring no more vain oblations; incense is an abomination unto me: the new moons and Sabbaths, the calling of assemblies, I cannot away with; it is iniquity, even the solemn meeting. Your new moons, and your appointed feasts my soul hateth. They are a trouble to me; I am weary to bear them; and when ye spread forth your hands I will hide mine eyes from you. Yea! when ye make many prayers, I will not hear. YOUR HANDS ARE FULL OF BLOOD; cease to do evil, learn to do well; seek judgment; relieve the oppressed; judge for the fatherless; plead for the widow.

The American church is guilty, when viewed in connection with what it is doing to uphold slavery; but it is superlatively guilty when viewed in its connection with its ability to abolish slavery.

The sin of which it is guilty is one of omission as well as of commission. Albert Barnes but uttered what the common sense of every man at all observant of the actual state of the case will receive as truth, when he declared that "There is no power out of the church that could sustain slavery an hour, if it were not sustained in it."

Let the religious press, the pulpit, the Sunday School, the conference meeting, the great ecclesiastical, missionary, Bible and tract associations of the land array their immense powers against slavery, and slave-holding; and the whole system of crime and blood would be scattered to the winds, and that they do not do this involves them in the most awful responsibility of which the mind can conceive.

In prosecuting the anti-slavery enterprise, we have been asked to spare the church, to spare the ministry; but how, we ask, could such a thing be done? We are met on the threshold of our efforts for the redemption of the slave, by the church and ministry of the country, in battle arrayed against us; and we are compelled to fight or flee. From what quarter, I beg to know, has proceeded a fire so deadly upon our ranks, during the last two years, as from the

Northern pulpit? As the champions of oppressors, the chosen men of American theology have appeared—men honored for their so-called piety, and their real learning. the LORDS of Buffalo, the SPRINGS of New York, the LATHROPS of Auburn, the COXES and SPENCERS of Brooklyn, the GANNETS and SHARPS of Boston, the DEWEYS of Washington, and other great religious lights of the land have, in utter denial of the authority of HIM by whom they professed to be called to the ministry, deliberately taught us, against the example of the Hebrews, and against the remonstrance of the Apostles, that we ought to obey man's law before the law of God.

My spirit wearies of such blasphemy; and how such men can be supported, as the "standing types and representatives of Jesus Christ," is a mystery which I leave others to penetrate. In speaking of the American church, however, let it be distinctly understood that I mean the great mass of the religious organizations of our land. There are exceptions, and I thank God that there are. Noble men may be found, scattered all over these Northern States, of whom Henry Ward Beecher, of Brooklyn; Samuel J. May, of Syracuse; and my esteemed friend (Rev. R. R. Raymond) on the platform, are shining examples; and let me say further, that, upon these men lies the duty to inspire our ranks with high religious faith and zeal, and to cheer us on in the great mission of the slave's redemption from his chains.

One is struck with the difference between the attitude of the American church towards the anti-slavery movement, and that occupied by the churches in England towards a similar movement in that country. There, the church, true to its mission of ameliorating, elevating and improving the condition of mankind, came forward promptly, bound up the wounds of the West Indian slave, and restored him to his liberty. There, the question of emancipation was a high religious question. It was demanded in the name of humanity, and according to the law of the living God. The Sharps, the Clarksons, the Wilberforces, the Buxtons, the Burchells, and the Knibbs were alike famous for their piety and for their philanthropy. The anti-slavery movement there was not an anti-church movement, for the reason that the church took its full share in prosecuting that movement: and the anti-slavery movement in this country will cease to be an anti-church movement, when the church of this country shall assume a favorable instead of a hostile position towards that movement.

Americans! your republican politics, not less than your republican union, are flagrantly inconsistent. You boast of your love of liberty, your superior civilization, and your pure Christianity, which the whole political power of the nation (as embodied in the two great political parties) is solemnly pledged to support and perpetuate the enslavement of three millions of your countrymen. You hurl your anathemas at the crowned headed tyrants of Russia and Austria and pride yourselves on your Democratic institutions, while you yourselves consent to be the mere tools and body-guards of the tyrants of Virginia and Carolina. You invite to your shores fugitives of oppression from abroad, honor them with banquets, greet them with ovations, cheer them, toast them, salute them, protect them, and pour out your money to them like water; but the fugitives from your own land you advertise, hunt, arrest, shoot, and kill. You glory in your refinement and your universal education; yet you maintain a system as barbarous and dreadful as ever stained the character of a nation—a system begun in avarice, supported in pride, and perpetuated in cruelty. You shed tears over fallen Hungary, and make the sad story of her wrongs the theme of your poets, statesmen, and orators, till your gallant sons are ready to fly to arms to vindicate her cause against the oppressor; but, in regard to the ten thousand wrongs of the American slave, you would enforce the strictest silence, and would hail him as an enemy of the nation who dares to make those wrongs the subject of public discourse! You are all on fire at the mention of liberty for France or for Ireland; but are as cold as an iceberg at the thought of liberty for the enslaved of America. You discourse eloquently on the dignity of labor; yet, you sustain a system which, in its very essence, casts a stigma upon labor. You can bare your bosom to the storm of British artillery to throw off a three-penny tax on tea; and yet wring the last hard earned farthing from the grasp of the black laborers of your country. You profess to believe "that, of one blood, God made all nations of men to dwell on the face of all the earth," and hath commanded all men, everywhere, to love one another; yet you notoriously hate (and glory in your hatred) all men whose skins are not colored like your own. You declare before the world, and are understood by the world to declare that you "hold these truths to be self-evident, that all men are created equal; and are endowed by their Creator with certain inalienable rights; and that among these are, life, liberty, and the pursuit of happiness;" and yet, you hold securely, in a bondage which, according to your own Thomas Jefferson, "is worse than ages of that which your fathers rose in rebellion to oppose," a seventh part of the inhabitants of your country.

Fellow-citizens, I will not enlarge further on your national inconsistencies. The existence of slavery in this country brands your republicanism as a sham, your humanity as a base pretense, and your Christianity as a lie. It destroys your moral power abroad: it corrupts your politicians at home. It saps the foundation of religion; it makes your name a hissing and a bye-word to a mocking earth. It is the antagonistic force in your government, the only thing that seriously disturbs and endangers your Union. It fetters your progress; it is the enemy of improvement; the deadly foe of education; it fosters pride, it breeds insolence; it promotes vice; it shelters crime; it is a curse to the earth that supports it; and yet you cling to it as if it were the sheet anchor of all your hopes. Oh! be warned! a horrible reptile is coiled up in your nation's bosom; the venomous creature is nursing at the tender breast of your youthful republic; for the love of God, tear away, and fling from you the hideous monster, and let the weight of twenty millions crush and destroy it forever!

But it is answered in reply to all this, that precisely what

I have now denounced is, in fact, guaranteed and sanctioned by the Constitution of the United States; that, the right to hold, and to hunt slaves is a part of that Constitution framed by the illustrious Fathers of this Republic.

Then, I dare to affirm, notwithstanding all I have said before, your fathers stooped, basely stooped

> To palter with us in a double sense:
> And keep the word of promise to the ear,
> But break it to the heart.

And instead of being the honest men I have before declared them to be, they were the veriest impostors that ever practised on mankind. This is the inevitable conclusion, and from it there is no escape; but I differ from those who charge this baseness on the framers of the Constitution of the United States. It is a slander upon their memory, at least, so I believe. There is not time now to argue the constitutional question at length; nor have I the ability to discuss it as it ought to be discussed. The subject has been handled with masterly power by Lysander Spooner, Esq., by William Goodell, by Samuel E. Sewall, Esq., and last, though not least, by Gerrit Smith, Esq. These gentlemen have, as I think, fully and clearly vindicated the Constitution from any design to support slavery for an hour.

Fellow-citizens! there is no matter in respect to which the people of the North have allowed themselves to be so ruinously imposed upon as that of the pro-slavery character of the Constitution. In that instrument I hold there is neither warrant, license, nor sanction of the hateful thing; but interpreted, as it ought to be interpreted, the Constitution is a GLORIOUS LIBERTY DOCUMENT. Read its preamble, consider its purposes. Is slavery among them? Is it at the gateway? or is it in the temple? it is neither. While I do not intend to argue this question on the present occasion, let me ask, if it be not somewhat singular that, if the Constitution were intended to be, by its framers and adopters, a slaveholding instrument, why neither slavery, slaveholding, nor slave can anywhere be found in it. What would be thought of an instrument, drawn up, legally drawn up, for the purpose of entitling the city of Rochester to a tract of land, in which no mention of land was made? Now, there are certain rules of interpretation for the proper understanding of all legal instruments. These rules are well established. They are plain, common-sense rules, such as you and I, and all of us, can understand and apply, without having passed years in the study of law. I scout the idea that the question of the constitutionality, or unconstitutionality of slavery, is not a question for the people. I hold that every American citizen has a right to form an opinion of the constitution, and to propagate that opinion, and to use all honorable means to make his opinion the prevailing one. Without this right, the liberty of an American citizen would be as insecure as that of a Frenchman. Ex-Vice-President Dallas tells us that the constitution is an object to which no American mind can be too attentive, and no American heart too devoted. He further says, the Constitution, in its words, is plain and intelligible, and is meant for the home-bred, unsophisticated understandings of our fellow-citizens. Senator Berrien tells us that the Constitution is the fundamental law, that which controls all others. The charter of our liberties, which every citizen has a personal interest in understanding thoroughly. The testimony of Senator Breese, Lewis Cass, and many others that might be named, who are everywhere esteemed as sound lawyers, so regard the constitution. I take it, therefore, that it is not presumption in a private citizen to form an opinion of that instrument.

Now, take the Constitution according to the plain reading, and I defy the presentation of a single pro-slavery clause in it. On the other hand, it will be found to contain principles and purposes, entirely hostile to the existence of slavery.

I have detained my audience entirely too long already. At some future period I will gladly avail myself of an opportunity to give this subject a full and fair discussion.

Allow me to say, in conclusion, notwithstanding the

dark picture I have this day presented, of the state of the nation, I do not despair of this country. There are forces in operation which must inevitably work the downfall of slavery. "The arm of the Lord is not shortened," and the doom of slavery is certain. I, therefore, leave off where I began, with hope. While drawing encouragement from "the Declaration of Independence," the great principles it contains, and the genius of American Institutions, my spirit is also cheered by the obvious tendencies of the age. Nations do not now stand in the same relation to each other that they did ages ago. No nation can now shut itself up from the surrounding world and trot round in the same old path of its fathers without interference. The time was when such could be done. Long established customs of hurtful character could formerly fence themselves in, and do their evil work with social impunity. Knowledge was then confined and enjoyed by the privileged few, and the multitude walked on in mental darkness. But a change has now come over the affairs of mankind. Walled cities and empires have become unfashionable. The arm of commerce has borne away the gates of the strong city. Intelligence is penetrating the darkest corners of the globe. It makes its pathway over and under the sea, as well as on the earth. Wind, steam, and lightning are its chartered agents. Oceans no longer divide, but link nations together. From Boston to London is now a holiday excursion. Space is comparatively annihilated. —Thoughts expressed on one side of the Atlantic are distinctly heard on the other.

The far off and almost fabulous Pacific rolls in grandeur at our feet. The Celestial Empire, the mystery of ages, is being solved. The fiat of the Almighty, "Let there be Light," has not yet spent its force. No abuse, no outrage whether in taste, sport or avarice, can now hide itself from the all-pervading light. The iron shoe, and crippled foot of China must be seen in contrast with nature. Africa must rise and put on her yet unwoven garment. "Ethiopia shall stretch out her hand unto God." In the fervent aspirations of William Lloyd Garrison, I say, and let every heart join in saying it:

God speed the year of jubilee
　　The wide world o'er!
When from their galling chains set free,
Th' oppress'd shall vilely bend the knee,
And wear the yoke of tyranny
　　Like brutes no more.
That year will come, and freedom's reign,
To man his plundered rights again
　　Restore.

God speed the day when human blood
　　Shall cease to flow!
In every clime be understood,
The claims of human brotherhood,
And each return for evil, good,
　　Not blow for blow;
That day will come all feuds to end,
And change into a faithful friend
　　Each foe.

God speed the hour, the glorious hour,
　　When none on earth
Shall exercise a lordly power,
Nor in a tyrant's presence cower;
But to all manhood's stature tower,
　　By equal birth!
That hour will come, to each, to all,
And from his prison-house, to thrall
　　Go forth.

Until that year, day, hour, arrive,
With head, and heart, and hand I'll strive, ·
To break the rod, and rend the gyve,
The spoiler of his prey deprive—
　　So witness Heaven!
And never from my chosen post,
Whate'er the peril or the cost,
　　Be driven.

Can there any good thing come out of Nazareth?[4]

ADAM CLAYTON POWELL

Almost 2,000 years ago, that question was a contemptuous inquiry in the book of John. "And Nathanael said unto Philip, 'Can there any good thing come out of Nazareth?' Philip saith, 'Come and see.'" Nazareth was the Mississippi of Galilee. There were no great artists or philosopher-kings or musicians. There was no center of learning such as Howard University. In this commencement of your life, the world will ask: Can there any good thing come out of Howard? As black students educated at America's finest black institution of higher learning, you are still second-class citizens.

A mere 100 years in the spectrum of time separates us from the history of slavery and a lifetime of indignities. Next year, on March 2, 1967, Howard will celebrate the centennial of its founding. Next year, on March 21, 1967, the Committee on Education and Labor of which I am the Chairman will also celebrate its 100th anniversary. How ironic that the Committee on Education and Labor which was formed immediately after the Civil War to help black slaves make the transition into freedom should have a black man 100 years later as its Chairman. One of the purposes of the Committee's founding was to take care of Howard Uni-

[4]The text of this speech was supplied by Congressman Adam Clayton Powell. This speech is reprinted with his permission.

versity. It is too late for you who are graduating to know this unless you plan to pursue graduate work here, but it is not too late for the faculty to know it: the Education and Labor Committee is in charge of Howard University. Howard, along with other Federal institutions such as St. Elizabeth's and Gallaudet College, is under the jurisdiction of my Committee. While both Howard and I as Chairman of this Committee will celebrate our 100 years together, joy of our success is tempered by the sobering fact that our status as black people has been denied first-class acceptance. Keith E. Baird, writing in the spring edition of "Freedom-ways", gives eloquent voice to these thoughts in his poem, "Nemesis":

> You snatched me from my land,
> Branded my body with your irons
> And my soul with the slave-name, 'Negro'
> (How devilish clever to spell it upper case
> And keep me always lower!)

To possess a black skin today in America means that if you are in Los Angeles driving your pregnant wife to a hospital, you'll be shot to death by a white policeman. A black skin means you are still a child, that all the white liberals who have helped you to take your first steps toward freedom and manhood now believe they own your soul, can manage your lives and control your civil rights organizations. Only SNICK has been able to resist the seductive blandishments of white liberals. So beware not only of Greeks bearing gifts, but colored men seeking loans and Northern white liberals!

At this graduation today, this is the reality of self you must face. Your graduation comes at a particularly critical period of the black man's searching re-assessment of who he is, what he should become and how he should become IT. The history of the last 25 years of the freedom struggle has been capsuled in only two concepts: integration and civil rights. During those years, our leaders—and black people are the only people who have "leaders"—other groups have politicians, statesmen, educators, financiers and businessmen —but during those years, our leaders drugged us with the LSD of integration. Instead of telling us to seek audacious power—more black power—instead of leading us in the pursuit of excellence, our leaders led us in the sterile chase of integration as an end in itself in the debasing notion that a few white skins sprinkled amongst us would somehow elevate the genetics of our development. As a result, ours was an integration of intellectual mediocrity, economic inferiority and political subservience. Like frightened children, we were afraid to eat the strong meat of human rights and instead sucked the milk of civil rights from the breasts of white liberals, black Uncle Toms and Aunt Jemimas. From the book of Hebrews, a diet of courage is offered to black people:

> For every one that useth milk is unskillful in the word of righteousness: for he is a babe. But strong meat belongeth to them that are of full age, even those who by reason of use have their senses exercised to discern both good and evil.

Historically, strong meat was too risky for most black people for it would have enabled them to discern both good and evil, the difference between civil rights and human rights.

I

Human rights are God-given. Civil rights are man-made. Civil rights has been that grand deception practiced by those who have not placed God first, who have not believed that God-given rights can empower the black man with superiority as well as equality.

II

Our life must be purposed to implement human rights:

*the right to be secure in one's person from the excessive abuses of the state and its law-enforcing officials.

*the right to freedom of choice of a job to feed one's family.

*the right to freedom of mobility of residence.

*the right to the finest education man's social order can provide.

*and most importantly, the right to share fully in the governing councils of the state as equal members of the body politic.

III

To demand these God-given human rights is to seek black power, what I call audacious power—the power to build black institutions of splendid achievement. Howard University was once well on its way toward becoming a lasting black institution of splendid achievement when it struggled to contain the intellectual excitement and dynamic creativity of such black scholars as Alain Locke, Sterling Brown, E. Franklin Frazier, Sam Dorsey, Eugene Holmes, James Nabrit and Rayford Logan—all on the campus at the same time. What glorious symbols they were on black creativity! But where are the black symbols of creativity of 1966? Where is the greatness of our yesteryears? Where are the sonnets black poets once sung of the black man's agony of life? Can any good thing come out of Howard today?

IV

There can and there must. I call today for a black renaissance at Howard University. Resurrect black creativity, not only in literature, history, law, poetry and English, but more so in mathematics, engineering, aerodynamics and nuclear physics. Like Nicodemus, Howard must be born again—born again in the image of black greatness gone before. Will one black woman here today dare to come forth as a pilgrim of God, a Sojourner Truth—as a black Moses, Harriet Tubman—or a Nannie Burroughs? Will one black man here today dare be a Denmark Vesey, a Nat Turner, a Frederick Douglass, a Marcus Garvey, a W. E. B. Du Bois or a Malcolm X? One with God is a majority. This divine oneness can restore Howard to the Glory of Charlie Houston whose classrooms were the womb of the civil rights movement—a womb that birthed a Thurgood Marshall. But the womb has aborted and the good thing which must come out of Howard must also come out of black people.

V

Ask yourselves that higher question: Can any good thing come of black people? We are the last revolutionaries in America—the last transfusion of freedom into the blood stream of democracy. Because we are, we must mobilize our wintry discontent to transform the cold heart and white face of this nation. Indeed, we must "drop our buckets" where we are. We must stop blaming "Whitey" for all our sins and oppressions and deal from situations with strength. Why sit down at the bargaining table with the white man when you have nothing with which to bargain? Why permit social workers and various Leagues and Associations to represent us when they are representing the decadent white power structure which pays their salaries, their rent and tells them what to say? Such men cannot possess the noble arrogance of power that inspires men, moves nations and decides the fate of mankind.

VI

I call for more arrogance of power among black people, but an arrogance of power that is God-inspired, God-led and God-daring. As Cassius said: "The fault, dear Brutus, is not in our stars, but in yourselves, that we are underlings. So, every bondman in his own hand bears the power to cancel his captivity." We can cancel the captivity of our souls and destroy the enslavement of our minds by refusing to compromise any of our human rights. The era of compromise for the black man is gone! Birmingham, Harlem and Watts have proved this. You cannot compromise man's right to be free, nor can you sit down and "reason together" whether man should have some rights today and full rights tomorrow. Let somebody reason with Mrs. Barbara Deadwyler in Los Angeles that a white policeman really did not intend to kill her black husband. Let somebody tell her that the passion of her love for her husband should bow to the reason of diphanous official alibis. Only God can reason with her and soothe her grief. And there is a "God who rules above with a hand of power and a heart of love, and if I'm right He'll fight my battle and I shall be free this day." This same God calls us first to the conference table, and His Son, when the word of reason was no longer heeded, went into the temple and "began to cast out those that sold." Those that sell black people down the river must be cast out. Those conference tables which defile the human spirit must be overturned. Conferences are for people who have time to contemplate the number of angels dancing on a civil rights pin. Conferences are for people who seek a postponement until tomorrow of a decision which screams for a solution today. Conferences are an extravagant orgy of therapy for the guilt-ridden and a purposeless exercise in dialectics for the lazy. America has been holding too many conferences, conducting too many seminars; writing too many books and articles about the black man and his right to freedom for over a century. This week, 3,000 black and white people will gather once again in our nation's capital to whisper words of futility into the hurricane of massive indifference. Certainly the Federal Government should cease to be a partner in this cruel, historic charade with the black man's rights. To fulfill these rights? Let us begin with first things first.

The largest single employer in the United States is the

Federal Government—2,574,000 employees. Yet, racial discrimination within the Government—more subtle, more sophisticated, more elegantly structured—continues almost as rampant as yesterday. The times have changed, but the system hasn't. Though racial persecution presses its crown of thorns on our brows, our faith in God must never falter. We must sustain that faith which helps us to cast off the leprosy of self-shame in our black skins and lift us up to the glorious healing power of belief in the excellence of black power. We must have the faith to build mighty black universities, black businesses and elect black men as governors, mayors and senators. Our faith must be sustained by our passion for dignity and our trust in God, not man's faithless reason in himself. What is easier—"to say to the sick of the palsy Thy sins be forgiven thee; or to say, Arise and take up thy bed and walk?" Black children of Howard, take up thy beds and walk into the new era of excellence. Arise, and walk into a new spirit of black pride. "Can there any good thing come out of Nazareth? Come and see, said Philip." Nathanael came and saw Jesus and the world felt, as he did, the power of his love and the beauty of his words. Can there any good thing come out of Howard University here today? "Come and see", you Howard graduates must say. "Come and see" us erect skyscrapers of economic accomplishment, scale mountains of educational excellence and live among the stars of audacious political power. "Come and see" us labor for the black masses—not the black leaders—but the black masses who have yearned for audacious leadership.

The Meaning of
Black Power[5]

MINISTER FRANKLIN FLORENCE

"To be a Negro in this country and to be conscious is to be in a rage almost all the time."

These are the words of James Baldwin, noted black author. I repeat: "To be"

These are trying days for black people. We have had three consecutive summers of violence and bloodshed in our cities. We have violence and bloodshed going on now in an immoral war in Vietnam. We have young strong black men who object to this war on religious grounds—like Mohammed Ali and they promptly strip him of his title. Dr. King was in a Southern jail all week because he stood up to Southern bigots. We have all powerful white America getting nervous over two little words—black power. After sticking and confining us into black ghettoes, what kind of power do they expect?—pink?

There has been a major shift in this country amongst our folks. We demonstrated in the late '50's and early '60's asking the white man for freedom now. Please Mr. White Man give us our freedom now. Today we are not talking to "the man"—we are talking to the brothers and sisters—we are calling on blacks to mobilize their social strength and gain power. This cry has nothing to do with black supremacy

[5]The text of this speech was supplied by Franklin Florence. This speech is reprinted with his permission.

161

but everything to do with black manhood and self-determination. Black is beautiful. Black is powerful. Black is here to stay. So you colored folks and you Negroes better catch up. Because some are going to get called what the black Ph.D. psychiatrist who appeared several years ago with Malcolm X at Harvard University on a T.V. program was called.

All night, the Negro psychiatrist had been saying that things weren't as bad as Malcolm said they were, that whites really loved Negroes, etc., until finally Malcolm couldn't stand it any longer. He leaned over to the psychiatrist and asked, "Have you got a Ph.D?" The psychiatrist smiled and admitted that he had one. Malcolm asked, "Do you know what white racists call Negro Ph.D's?" The psychiatrist was taken back a bit, but said, "No, I don't. What do they call us?" Malcolm answered "*Niggers!*"

"We wish to plead our own cause. Too long have others spoken for us." CUA has come a long way in one year. Your leadership has conducted excellent programs in opportunities drive, in housing, in battling the school board, in fighting for the poor and needed recreational services, for standing behind your affiliates on street lights, community maintenance and other local issues.

You are beginning to get down to business now. You got the man scared of you. You forced him to withdraw his injunction and to agree with what you asked him to sign in the first place.

But you have just begun on getting jobs. Make the man downtown do what he ought to do anyway. Demand your share of those Christmas jobs in the department stores—start next week and demand them. Don't go down there begging, hat in hand.

We had a few Negroes in Rochester who said you can't win with the big Boys. They said "go slow"; they said, "they are too big"; they said, "the name of the game is to win and you can't win with Kodak"; they said, "be nice, be polite". Well, we blacks in Rochester were tired of that tea sipping, safe Tom approach. We told those house Negroes to go back and tell Master Charlie, Master Kodak that we were going to overexpose their film and them with it. Well, you know what happened. FIGHT in Rochester like CUA in Kansas City made them sign up. And you better start signing up Bendix, General Motors, Ford, Western Electric, the insurance companies and TWA. But do me a favor—don't start on TWA until I get flown back to Rochester.

Now let me tell you something about those who run downtown and who run big business. They are trying desperately to convince us that high school diplomas are essential for getting hired. That there is some relationship between graduating out of high school and getting a job. Sure there is a relationship because they have set it up that way—no high school—no job. Black Ph.D's make nearly one-half of what white Ph.D's make. Black unemployment increases; white unemployment decreases. I could go on.

Let's look at it. During World War II our country took sharecroppers and turned them into shipbuilders in a few months because of a labor shortage; our country took domestics and turned them into riveters in a few months because of a labor shortage.

I maintain that our country can take drop-outs, drop-ins, you name it—and teach them skills and give them decent jobs. We can teach them to be soldiers and to kill for a living—let's teach them to be solderers, electronic wirers, salesmen, businessmen. Private industry can do it—they have the money, they have the know-how.

Japan and West Germany have rebuilt from the ashes a highly industrialized, technical and successful economy using poor uneducated workers—why can't our leaders—I'll tell you why—because they think we are sick. That our children are inferior, that Negroes can't be taught skills.

Don't buy this line—They have waived the rules for the Irish, the Germans, the Anglo-Saxons, the Italians, the Puerto Rican and now we have to make them waive it for us. Organize and make them sign agreements. Organize and make them deal with you for jobs. We owe it to our children.

I read a couple of months ago that LBJ was in Kansas City talking to Police Chiefs from all over the world. I don't know about you but I didn't like what I heard. We blacks have been hitting hard on police brutality and police discrimination throughout the country. Because of this Police Chiefs are now coming up with smoke screen "human relations" and "internal affairs units" in order to take the heat off themselves. Watch out they are trying to give us a whitewash. Hold Chief Kelley responsible for what happens in your community. Hold Chief Kelley responsible for brutality. Hold Chief Kelley answerable to the black community. The whites hold him responsible for what happens in their communities.

Negroes are no longer asking for equality—we are *demanding* it. The black man is no longer begging anybody for anything, and you know why not—BECAUSE BLACKS HAVE DISCOVERED POWER, P - O - W - E - R. And we plans to use it.

POWER. The "P" stands for *Persistence*: You got to wear them down, like you did 7-Up, like we did Kodak.

The "O" stands for *Organization*: in Rochester, that's spelled F-I-G-H-T. In Kansas City that's spelled C-U-A.

The "W" stands for *Whitey*—He's got all the power; it's called the white power structure. You have to get your share of it. It won't be given—you just have to take it.

The "E" in "POWER" is for *Effort*: That's the sweat and heart-aches you have to invest—and believe me CUA has one good hard year of *effort* in it.

The "R" in "POWER" is for *Results*. The name of the game is win, and you proved it with Vess, Manor, Wonder Bread, Tastee, and just yesterday with 7-Up.

So, POWER has to do with persistence, organization, whitey, effort, and results. CUA has in this first year developed a good set of muscles, and CUA must be willing to use those muscles to increase its power base.

CUA must become more powerful. The battles will be even tougher than the 7-Up one.

It is a good healthy sign that so many of your brothers are candidates for office here this evening. It means that you have strong leadership, and you are going to need that during these next years. You are going to need a strong president, and you are also going to need the loyal support of everyone. A president alone does not make an organization. I am confident that the president you elect tonight will give his undying loyalty and efforts to move CUA forward. I am confident that the next year will be even greater than the last.

And to those hundreds of volunteers and workers—and to the black youth—probably the most important factor in our future—and to the black common man who wants to see things change—two words of advice:

The first is something Saul Alinsky said to me three years ago: "Minister Florence, never wear your best trousers to go out and fight for freedom and battle for justice."

And I say tonight freedom and justice are not gifts— you must take them—rise up, you mighty black people— organize and take power. In that is your dignity—your self-respect—your honor—your future—your hope.

Political Struggle
in America[6]

ELDRIDGE CLEAVER

I think the first thing we have to realize, really get into
our minds, is that it is a reality when you hear people say
that there's a "black colony" and a "white mother country."
I think you really have to get that distinction clear in your
minds in order to understand that there are two different
sets of political dynamics functioning in this country. If you
don't make that distinction, then a lot of the activities going
on in this country will be non-sensical. For instance, if
there's a homogeneous country and everyone here is a
citizen of that country, when it comes to participating in
the politics of this country, it makes a lot of sense to insist
that black people participate in electoral politics and all the
other forms of politics as we have known them. But if you
accept the analysis that the black colony is separate and
distinct from the mother country, then a lot of other forms
of political struggle are indicated.

I think that most black revolutionaries or militants or
what have you have generally accepted this distinction. A
lot of people seem reluctant to accept this distinction. I
know that in your education you were given to believe the
melting pot theory, that people have come from all over the
world and they've been put into this big pot and they've
been melted into American citizens. In terms of the white
immigrants who came to this country, this is more or less

6This speech is reprinted from the *Black Panther*, March 16, 1968.

true. But in this stew that's been produced by these years and years of stirring the pot, you'll find that the black elements, the black components have not blended well with the rest of the ingredients. And this is so because of the forms of oppression that have been generated—black people have been blocked out of this, and blocked out of that, and not allowed to participate in this, and excluded from that. This has created a psychology in black people where they have now turned all the negative exclusions to their advantage.

I mean the same things that were used to our disadvantage are now being turned around to our advantage. The whole thing about condemning blackness and developing an inferior image of everything black has now been turned completely around because I think the slogan of Black Power was a recognition of the change in the psychology of black people, that in fact they have seized upon their blackness and rallied around the elements or the points at which they were oppressed. They have turned the focal point of the oppression into the focal point of the struggle for national liberation.

Now, when people decide in their own minds that they are going to separate themselves from a country or from a political situation, a lot of dynamics and a lot of directions flow from that basic distinction. For example, people are talking these days about going to the United Nations and seeking membership in the United Nations for Afro-America. And when you look at the criteria for nationhood, you'll find that the only place that black people fall short in terms of this standard is the one where the land question comes up. They say that a nation is defined as a people sharing a common culture, a common language, a common history, and a common land situation. Now, that land question was a hang-up for a long time, simply because the black people in this country were dispersed throughout the population of the mother country. People couldn't begin to deal with the question of how to build a nation on someone else's land. It presents a very sticky problem.

In the history of the liberation struggle in this country,

the two outstanding efforts that we remember in history were the Marcus Garvey movement and the Nation of Islam under Elijah Muhammed. I consider their fundamental mistake was that they projected goals that they were unable to fulfill. Marcus Garvey said that he was going to take black people back to Africa. In fact, he wasn't in a position to do that, technically speaking in terms of resources. It falls down to a question of resources, because I think that if Marcus Garvey had been able to come over here with enough ships and enough technical resources, he would have succeeded, because he did have a very tight grip on the minds and imaginations of black people, and he could have had enough of them with him to make his dream a reality. Elijah Muhammed said that he wanted to have a part of this country, that he would accept some of these states. Well, the way he approached the question I think, was sure to doom it to be unfulfilled because he was asking the white power structure to give him several states. He offered no alternative means of obtaining these states other than come down from the sky and give them to us. Well, black people have been waiting for help to come from abroad and from the sky, from underground, and from anywhere, and it hasn't come. So that we began to feel that we were in a bag where nothing could happen.

The beautiful thing about the slogan Black Power was that it implemented the dictum laid down by Kwame Nkrumah, in which he said, "Seek ye first the political kingdom, and other things will be added unto you." It's very important to realize that in moving to gain power, you do not conceal or repudiate the land question, you hold it in abeyance. What you're saying is that we must first get ourselves organized, and then we can get some of this land. It's very important to realize that 20,000,000 people or 30,000,000 people, what have you—we're going to have to take a count because the government has been lying to us about everything else they do so we can assume that they are lying about that, so we can say that there might be 30,000,000, 40,000,000 we might even be a majority, I don't know; but I am quite sure that there are more than the 20,000,000 that the government wants to give us. But, we can say that it's possible to organize 20,000,000 or 30,000,000 people right here. Even though we are dispersed throughout the mother country, it is possible to set up political forms where we can have representatives in the full sense of the word, like ambassadors going to other countries.

You can see from the experience of Malcolm and from the experience of Stokely that governments around the world are hip enough to the political realities of our situation to recognize and to accept our representatives in every sense of the word. I mean, Stokely Carmichael, when he went to Havana, received the same respect, or maybe even a little more, as delegates from other countries. Black people recognize this and they know that there is a way through the international machinery to cope with the situation.

I think it's very important to realize that there is a way to move. So that today black people are talking about going to the United Nations, asking the United Nations for a UN supervised plebiscite throughout the colony. Black people have never been able through any mechanism to express what their will is. People have come along and spoken in the name of black people; they have said that black people want to be integrated; they have said black people want to be separated; but no where at no time have black people been given the chance to register their own position. I think it's very important that we decide this once and for all, because as black people we are able to wage a campaign on this subject: do you want to be a part of America, do you want to be integrated into America, or do you want to be separated from America, do you want to be a nation, do you want to have your ambassadors, your representatives seated in the United Nations, as a full member of the General Assembly, do you want to have your ambassadors accepted around the world? I think it would be very hard for the black people to say no, particularly when the argument of the government is going to be that black people don't need those things because they are already American citizens. Because then we come back and say, Well, if we're citizens, what about this, and what about that? And, at the very least, what it will do is to put tremendous pressure on the Babylonians, and they need all the pressure we can give them.

Now, a lot of people don't want to see this country and its structure basically change. They want to think the United States of America is an eternal entity. When you look at history, you'll find that great empires have had their boundaries changed, have had their political structures rearranged, and some of them, like Rome, lasted for 500, 600 years, and the people thought nothing could ever destroy this. It's gone. The Egyptian Empire—all the empires as you look down through history, you will find that a day of reckoning came down and the whole situation was rearranged. Americans cannot envision a situation where the same thing could happen here. I think that black people have already envisioned that this, in fact, could happen, because if we were to get organized in this fashion and then be able to bring international leverage against the United States, we could have those questions decided in our favor in an international forum. I think that by then Mao Tse-tung would be at the UN, I think he would vote for us, I don't think he would sustain LBJ's argument. I think that Fidel Castro would vote for us. I think Charles De Gaulle may say something about that. I don't think he would just turn thumbs down on us, so that there are a lot of areas that we have to get into and explore. Now what that means is that there are realities out here today and will be in the future.

One thing about the coalition with the Peace and Freedom Party: we approached this whole thing from the point of view of international realtions. We feel that our coalition is part of our foreign policy. That is how we look at it, that is how we are moving on it and thinking about it.

A lot of people feel just as Mike Parker said: We are endangering them as well as ourselves by coalescing with the white radicals, particularly here in Berkeley. Berkeley, as far as we can see, has a foul reputation among a lot of black cats, especially black cats associated with the NCNP. Bobby Seale, myself, and several other members of the Black Panther Party spent about a week in Los Angeles, and we were put through a lot of changes by black cats who didn't relate to the Peace and Freedom Party. They told us rather frankly that we had become tools of the white racists who had refused to accept the 50% bit in Chicago and they wanted to know what we were trying to do, were we trying to undercut what other blacks were trying to around the country? Our reply to that was that we had made a functional coalition with the Peace and Freedom Party and that we feel that we have 100% say so over our affairs. I mean we don't allow Mike Parker and Bob Avakian to come in and dictate to us what is going to happen in terms of what we want to do. They have not tried to do that, and they are not going to try, and they had better not try. And in the same way, we do not come in and try to dictate to them what they are going to do, although we have been accused of that, but that is not the way it goes.

We recognize that we have a powerful interest in seeing a white radical movement develop into something that we can relate to. There are many things that we cannot do by ourselves. And then, there are many things that the white radical movement cannot do by itself. So we recognize that, and we are not going to be running around trying to stab each other in the back, or put each other in trickbags. It is not going to work from our point of view and we hope it won't work from your point of view because we have an interest in seeing that you develop a stable organization and a stable movement.

Now, one very important thing that we are working towards is how to unify the black population in this country within a national structure. The structure has to be inclusive enough to pull in all black people. In the past, when a new organization came on the scene, it sought to eliminate existing organizations. It was going to move every other organization out and it was going to take over and do this thing. We say that this is a mistake. What we have done is worked out a merger with SNCC. The Black Panther Party for Self-Defense and SNCC are going to merge into a functional organization that can move nationally. We are moving into a period now where the Black Panther Party for Self-Defense has consolidated enough of a base to move things nationally. SNCC has already established national contact as well as international contact.

It is very important to realize that SNCC is composed virtually of black hippies, you might say, of black college students who have dropped out of the black middle class. And because that is their origin and that is where they came from, they cannot relate to the black brother on the block in a political fashion. They can relate to him, they can talk to him, they can communicate with him much better than, say, Roy Wilkins ever could. But, they are not able to move him *en masse* to the point where he could be organized and involved in political functions.

Now, the beauty and the genius of what Bobby Seale and Huey Newton have done is that they are able to move the last man on the totem pole. That is very important, because until that man can move, we really can't do that thing. SNCC has seen that the Black Panther Party is able to get to that man. So what they have done is made their apparatus available to us and there's no hangup; we can move into that. Most people don't know this, but a lot of the rhetoric you hear from Stokely Carmichael and Rap Brown these days, especially when Rap Brown first started speaking, was adopted precisely because they had come to the West Coast and spent a little time with the Black Panthers out here. That is very important, and if you see them you ask them to tell you about that, that they were greatly influenced by the Panthers. I mean that their lines were already moving in that direction because of the political pressures they were forced to deal with, but they hadn't yet made that step, they hadn't taken that leap. But coming out here and seeing the Panthers moving, seeing brothers carrying guns on the street, talking about the gun, violence, and revolution had a certain impact on their minds and they went back talking about that. So now we can say that SNCC—actually, I shouldn't even be going into this until February 17th at the Oakland Auditorium. This is when we are going to do this officially. I think it is very important that you be there so that you can see and hear for yourself what these pepole have to say, unless you want to depend on the newspapers, and you really don't want to get into that. So, let's just say that we are involved in trying to create models in the vanguard set so that people around the country will see how we can move.

Now, we have done two important things, I think. One, we have made this coalition with the Peace and Freedom Party; and two, we have merged with SNCC. When people look at that they can say that in the Era of Black Power, we have got to merge and merge into larger units until we have a national structure. In terms of our relationship with the white community, we can move with functional coalitions.

It is very important that we all hold up our end of the bargain—and don't think that by using us you can get away with something, because, in fact, you will only destroy what you are trying to build for yourself. Black people have only one way to protect themselves, particularly politically, and that is to be capable of implementing and inflicting a political consequence. If we cannot inflict a political consequence, then we will in fact become nothing. So, that if the Peace and Freedom Party ever tries to misuse us, we have to be in a position to hurt the Peace and Freedom Party. We have to keep the political relationship such that if we were to pull out of it, that would be very costly to the Peace and Freedom Party. We must maintain that, we must be able to inflict a consequence, and we intend to be able to do that, and it is very important that that happens. White radicals who are like the vanguard in the white community should recognize that and then move to help us get in that position —because without that you are not going to be able to convince people that they should even relate to this whole effort.

As Mike Parker said, we are also catching a lot of hell— the word is purgatory, rather, it is not hell—about this coalition. Because a lot of people have begun to feel that we can be trusted, they have taken a wait-and-see attitude to find out how this coalition comes down, to see if we, in fact, do become puppets. People all around the country are asking—if you could look at our mail or listen to our phone calls—you would know about all the people who have asked, "Hey, what is this you are doing out there? What do you think you're doing, man, explain that to me." We feel that we are able to explain that, and as I said, Bobby is going to be going on a nation-wide tour and is going to be explaining that, I am going on a nation-wide tour and other members of the Party are going to be going on these tours. We are going to be explaining it and SNCC is going to be explaining it, and I think that we are going to be able to do it. It is very important that the Peace and Freedom Party be able to relate to that, because when we move nationally we will have to talk about the Peace and Freedom Party and then they will have grounds for moving into areas that we have already organized. So it is going to become extremely important that we realize what we are doing. And the thing that we need from the white mother country is technical assistance—technical assistance to the colony, dig it?

I think we have a good thing going. I want to see it continue to develop and broaden and deepen because we are all involved in this and there is no way out. We have got to do it, because time is against us, a lot of people are against us, and I know that I am out of time, so I think I will cool it right here.

Free Huey[7]

BOBBY SEALE

Brothers and Sisters, tonight I want to have the chance to tell you in large mass something about Brother Huey P. Newton; a black man that I've been knowing for about eight years; a black man who first introduced me to what black nationalism was all about; a black man that I've been closely associated with for the last three years in the organizing of a black people's party on a level that dealt with black people's problems. To explain to you who Brother Huey P. Newton is in his soul, I've got to explain to you also *your* soul, your needs, your political desires and needs, because that is *Huey's* soul.

You know, I met Huey and he told me that he first learned how to read good when he was about 16. He was coming out of high school, and one of these counselors in school told him be could not be college material. Huey got mad. He didn't like no *white* man telling him he couldn't do. And Huey learned how to read. And Huey went to Oakland City College, and I went right there with him, and Huey got a 4.0—that's an A in sociology, psychology, political science, law, he run it on down, he got A's all the way through, and he said, "Later for the Man, I *know* what I can do."

Huey learned the need for black people to develop a

[7]This speech is reprinted from the *Black Panther*, March 16, 1968.

perspective and an understanding of our oppressive conditions. Now, when we first organized the Black Panther Party for Self Defense, Huey said, "Bobby, we're going to draw up a basic platform, just basic, that black people can read." He said, "We don't want to go real elaborate, with all these essays and dissertations and all that stuff, 'cause the brother's gonna look at that and he's gonna say, "Man, I don't have time for that, I gotta go and see what I can do for myself." Just a basic platform that the mothers who struggled hard to raise us, that the fathers who worked hard to feed us, that the young brothers in school, who come out of school semi-literate, saying and reading broken words that all of these can read. He said we want a basic platform to outline black people's basic political desires and needs. So we sit down.

Huey said, First we want freedom, we want power to determine the destiny of our black communities. No. 2: We want full employment for our people. No. 3: We want housing fit for shelter of human beings. No. 4: We want all black men to be exempt from military service. No. 5: We want decent education for our black people in our communities that teaches us the true nature of this decadent, racist society, and that teaches black people and our young black brothers and sisters their place in the society, for if they don't know their place in society and in the world, they can't relate to anything else. No. 6: We want an end to the robbery by the white racist businessman of black people in their community. No. 7: We want an IMMEDIATE end to police brutality and *murder* of black people. No. 8: We want all black men held in city, county, state, and federal jails and prisons to be released because they have not had a fair trial because they've been tried by *all white juries*, and that's just like being tried in Nazi Germany, being a Jew. No. 9: We want black people when brought to trial to be tried by members of their peer group; and a peer being one who comes from the same economic, social, religious, historical and racial background; that, in fact, black people, if the United States government and the local courts did this, they would have to choose *black* people from the *black* community to sit up on the jury. They would have to choose some of them mothers who have been working 20 long hard hours a day, as my mother has done. They'd have to choose some of them hard working fathers, they'd have to choose some of those brothers who stand on the block out there wondering where they're going to get a gig. They're going to choose these black people. And No. 10: Huey said, let's summarize it: "We want land, we want bread, we want housing, we want clothing, we want education, we want justice, and we want peace."

This is a basic platform. In case you never knew it or not, all the things you've heard in the press, of all the derogatory statements that have been made in the press about Brother Huey P. Newton and I, that was all to guide you *away* from seeing this basic platform that Huey was talking about for his own people! We have to learn to look through the white press. We have to learn to see what's going on.

Now, out of this platform, Huey P. Newton realized that it was necessary for us to start working on these points, these ten points, *practically*. Remember No. 7, "We want an IMMEDIATE end to Police brutality and murder of black people?" That's very important. Huey did a year and one half in law school after he got out of Merritt College, with an Associate Arts Degree in Social Sciences. Huey articulated to brothers on the block and he articulated in a manner where they understood what their rights were in law, and how in fact, we could exercise a position in the black community to begin to show black people how we could defend ourselves on point no. 7.

Now the papers called the organization hoodlums and thugs. Now I'm gonna show you how smart Brother Huey is when he planned Sacramento. He said, Now, the papers gon call us thugs and hoodlums. A lot of people ain't gon know what's happening. But the brothers on the block, who the man's been calling thugs and hoodlums for four hundred years, gon say, "Them some out of sight thugs and hoodlums up there!" The brothers on the block gon say, 'Who *is* these THUGS and HOODLUMS? In fact, I know George Dowell, in fact, I know Bobby Hutton, hey man, I know that dude over there, hey man, what you cats doing with them rods?" In other words, when the man calls us "nigger" for four hundred years with all its derogatory connotations, Huey was smart enough to know that black people were going to say, "Well, they've been calling us niggers, thugs, and hoodlums for four hundred years, that ain't gon hurt *me*, I'm going to check out what these brothers is doing!" The insight that Huey had in knowing how to deal with organizing black people, and know how to bring black people together. Now, at the same time, many of our older brothers and sisters were gonna say, "They must really be thugs and hoodlums. *But*, they're talking about police brutality," and many of you have related in one way or another through relatives or members of your family, etc. to the conditions and how police brutality is, and you would sit in your homes and say, "Yeah, we should have did it four hundred years ago, we should have got out there and started defending ourselves in this fashion."

Now, at the same time, many people get the notion that we were supposed to go out in the streets with five hundred black people lined up with guns and shoot it out with a thousand policemen—no, this wasn't the case at all. This wasn't the case at all. On the contrary, every black man in his home, has a right to defend his home. It was necessary to bring to black people the understanding that they were going to have to stand in defense of life, of community, of your children, of your mothers, of our young, we have to defend ourselves, starting with point no. 7. Because we don't *end* self-defense there. Because, Huey said, we still have to defend ourself against the gross, unemployment we are subjected to, against the indecent housing we are subjected to, against the indecent education that we're getting, against the way black men are drafted off into the military service after we fought in the Civil War 186,000 in World War I, 350,000, in World War II, 850,000 and all the way down to the Korean Conflict and now that jive Vietnam War and they're drafting our black brothers off the block at 90 miles an hour., Huey said, "Un-hu!" And they been promising us freedom for all these years, Huey said, "No, that's a very, very important point!" Every black man and his house should be against the war in Vietnam, got to be against the war in Vietnam because THEY'RE KILLING OUR BLACK BROTHERS OVER THERE!

Huey brought it down to a practical level, for us to try and understand. When Huey organized these brothers, he didn't just run 'em out in the street with zero understanding. Huey sit those brothers down and taught them 12 points of law and how to exercise their constitutional right. Huey sit those brothers down and talked to them. Huey taught those brothers that it wasn't the gun that was dangerous, it's the person *behind* it, that is dangerous. It's very important. Huey taught the brothers safety of those weapons. You haven't heard of one Black Panther shooting another Black Panther accidentally. But from the information and one appearance in court, Charles Garry, the lawyer, he's saying that one cop down there shot the other cop where Huey was.

Now look, the Black Panther Party is a revolutionary party. Revolution means that we got to get down to the nitty gritty and change this situation that we're in and don't miss any nits or any grits—that's very, very important. All the time. We also struggled for—to show you that it wasn't only the cops, but we had to deal with many other things, like—a street light, at Market and 55th Street. Three kids coming from Washington School had been killed two years prior. We got with the Poverty Program and said there's gotta be a street light here, and if there don't be a street light here the Panthers are going to get right out here and we're going to protest. They said, "Well, you'll tie the traffic up," and we said, "Well, the traffic's just gon get tied up—our little kids ain't gon get killed!" We shot a petition in conjunction with members of the area there to the City Council and they sent something back talking about "Well, we can't put one up til late 1968." We said, "No, we're gon have to change the situation now, not later—not late 1968. Well, the street light is up early 1968 now—they don't like the Panthers messing with them no kinda way, you dig.

I'm saying that these programs have to involve not only the members of the Black Panther Party, they have to involve *you*, as a whole. That's when the Black Panther Party for Self Defense starts coming to the black community and starts knocking on your doors, starts leaving you literature, and giving you information concerning the fact that our black brother Huey P. Newton has got to be set free—we want you to come down to the local defense fund committee for Huey and work and operate, if you want to work in the Black Panther Party you gonna be doing the same thing 'cause with the Huey P. Newton Defense Fund, it's all together, every last one black person in here has got to stand up right now and say he's a member of the Defense fund for Huey P. Newton! Now I want to see how many black people gon stand up now. Let's Free Huey! I'll give you a hand. I'm gonna give you a hand. YOU'RE THE HEROES! Huey's gonna *call* you the heroes. (YOU'RE THE HEROES)

Black brothers and sisters, we're gon have some unity here. We're gonna have some unity behind Brother Huey P. Newton because Huey was trying to unify us to solve all of our problems. Huey was for us. The man has got Huey chained up—watch where I point my finder—Did you see the building over there—right in back—He's chained up in *jail*, right across the street! When we announce Huey's court date appearance *you be there* for an hour or an hour an one half and show a standing support that we should have Huey P. Newton set free! Be there brothers and sisters, and tell your friends and explain to black people what Huey P. Newton was doing with the Black Panther Party for Self Defense, what kind of organization it was. Let people know that it is necessary, that we must unify on *all* levels. And *all* the areas of oppression, we must deal with them. That right here in the confines of racist America, racism must be stopped.

When a man walks up and says that we are anti-white

I scratch my head, I say "anti-white? What does he mean by that?" He says, "Well I mean you hate white people." I say, "Me, hate a white person?" I say, "Wait a minute, man—let's back up a little bit." That's your game, that's the Ku Klux Klan's game. To hate me and murder me because of the color of my skin. I wouldn't murder a person or brutalize him because of the color of his skin. Yeah, we HATE something alright. We hate the OPPRESSION that we live in. We hate cops beating black people over their heads and murdering them. THAT'S what we hate. If you got enough energy to sit down and hate a white person *just* because of the color of his skin, you're wasting a lot of energy. You'd better take some of that same energy and put it in some motion and start dealing with those oppressive conditions and you gon find out *just* what you hate. And what you gon stop.

Black People, we are organizing to STOP racism, you dig it. When you stop racism, you stop brutality and murder of black people by the racist, occupying army in our black community, that's what we're gonna stop. What's being DONE to us. You dig it! Can you dig the white power structure and its racist police force and how they've escalated the situation, that before Watts, there was 1300 cops now there's 6000 cops patrolling black people, that in Oakland, they had 350 cops just three and a half years ago, now they got a thousand cops patrolling black people? San Francisco's doubled its police force, and every major metropolis where black people live all across this country they've doubled and tripled and quadrupled their police force and equipped them with tanks, all kinds of artillery—un, uh we got to stop it brothers, let's unify!

Brother Huey was concerned about the nation and the survival of black people. That's why tonight and your standing support; We are ALL gonna be concerned about him. I saw a picture in the paper where it showed one sister holding a sign that said, "Come See About Huey." And so every court date I want everybody in this house to come see about Huey at that courthouse 'cause we gonna free him,

FREE HUEY HUEY, come on FREE HUEY! FREE HUEY! FREE HUEY! FREE HUEY!

Now, before we go any further, there are some sisters here—there are a lot more things I want to say to you—maybe I should say a few more things to you. Maybe I should give some more information. Yeath, I feel inadequate not doing that. I do really feel inadequate not doing that. Yeah, let's get on down to the nitty gritty like I said. And, I'm gonna get the griys, too, brother, come on and look—I'm with you. Let's go into a little detail.

When a young black man comes out of any of these high schools around here, he's not taught—now watch how this power structure tricks you—one iota about the white man's law. And he plasters on TV that we're supposed to respect the law. Then some racist cop—Brother Carmichael done hipped me to how the racist cops come into the situation up here—because he says all down in the Post Office down South they got brochures announcing jobs for cops in Oakland, San Francisco, Los Angeles, and all these racist pigs up here—See? And this same pig that comes from way down there, and also coming up here with his other brothers who *been* up here, getting together out in the streets, and walks up to a young black man and says, "Boy," or "Nigger, where you going?" And a cop either reaches for his billy club, or reaches for his pistol, and the brother don't see no respect for him as a human being. What else can the brother do, at that point, but to say, "Man, if you hit me with that club, I'm sorry, I ain't going for it." You see, now look, what happens here? The brother winds up busted. He gets put in jail. You read some junk in the paper. On one occasion or another, he is killed or murdered—he allegedly was burglarizing something. Which is a bunch of bunk. That's the way the cops cover up their story. Or, "He assaulted me" the cop say, and it's passed off.

But we got to learn to see through what's happening out there. When we go to the courts, where this brother done got busted—you walk up in Municipal Court, and I know a lot of y'all been up there, walk up in there, you know what you see in that court. Ninety per cent black people and the other ones who ain't black are poor whites and our Mexican brothers. You catch it? These cops are not in Piedmont brutalizing and intimidating white people. They are not in the Berkeley Hills brutalizing and intimidating white people. They are down in the *black ghettos* where our communities are, where we have to have the power to determine the destiny of our own community. Why shouldn't we have our own police station where we set up operations and organizations through the churches and everything else to choose our own policemen? Cause when we choose our own policemen, and we make the rule that that policeman has to live in our community, he ain't gonna be brutalizing too much if he have to come back and sleep there that night!

These are the teachings of the Minister of Defense of the Black Panther Party, Huey P. Newton. They're basic. And here, whether you know it or not, is where you start dealing with the black revolution. When Huey said, "Every black man, put a shotgun in your home." Do you remember about the Smith family and how the cops raided the home of the Smith family? Do you remember how one of the sons had a white friend who came down to their basement where they had a pool table and he just walked in with his young family and some cops saw him go down there? These cops all got together, radioed some more cops, and busted in the house. They said they thought it was prostitution. You know what they did? They walked in the house on a man, his wife, and his children, brutalized and beat a whole family up from child to mother to father— broken arms, crushed skulls—and then the cops turned around and charged the unarmed family with "assault on a police officer!" What kind of crap is that? That's why a black man needs a shotgun in his home! It's very important.

You understand what I am talking about? This is very, very important for us to recognize, and that once when we organize in this fashion, right there in our *homes*, we're talking about *power* in our *community* to control our communities, you know.

And once we let the man know, Say, Look, we're armed

from block to block, we're going to patrol you from our
windows, and we're not gonna have you brutalizing none
of our people in the streets. Do you realize what kind of
power black people have then? Because then you begin to
neutralize that police force, cause them cops are gonna start
to riding shaky and scared. In fact, we're in a position then
to demand that they *withdraw* from our communities because they *occupy* our community just like a foreign troop
occupying territory. It's very important to understand.

This is the political teachings of Brother Huey. And you
see how basic it is? It's not hard to understand at all. Every-
time the power structure makes a political decision upon
any group of people, if the people disagree with the political
decision the power structure has made upon them, then the
power structure gets guns and force and billy clubs and
starts doubling and tripling police forces and National
Guard to make you *accept* those political decisions made
when you try to disagree. The Vietnamese have had political
decisions made upon them and their country and they have
disagreed with them. So, they said, Naw, we're going to
defend ourselves right here on our land, and we want you
to withdraw from our land.

Now, we can parallel the situation, when we see all
these racist cops off in our community the way they are.
But remember, that's only *point 7*, of the program. But here
is the *key* in terms of dealing with what the *real* power is.
Power starts *here*. When people try to say Green Power is
where its at, let me hip you to a little something that
Brother Huey P. Newton knew. During the Civil War, there
was the North and there was the South. The North had
Yankee money, green power, supposedly. He said, but when
the North outmaneuvered the South, and the North had all
the guns, *they* said, Your money ain't no good no more.
You don't even have no so-called green power. So, I'm saying that the money is only a tool by which you manipulate
the power. That's all. The real power is manifested in the
police forces, national guardsmen, these racists who come
down to occupy black people in their community, and

maintain the oppression to try to make us stoop. We in our homes, and I'm saying every black brother in his house, every last one of you, put a shotgun in your home, put a shotgun in your home. That's necessary.

We will begin to deal in politics that way. Because, Huey, also says, that politics is war without bloodshed but war is politics *with* bloodshed. Let's get down to the nitty gritty here and see what's happening here. A contradiction between a group of people, or might we say contractions, disagreements, etc., you have two kinds of contradictions: antagonistic contradictions, where there's fighting and there's bloodshed, and non-antagonistic contradictions, where there's arguing and debating. Now I'm pretty sure that black people would prefer to have in dealing with positive politics non-antagonistic contradictions. But what's happened here? When the man escalates his police force, doubles and triples them, and is murdering black people in their community, shooting them, down, that ain't non-antagonistic, that's very antagonistic cause he's shedding our blood, he has made war upon us. This is very, very important, to understand where politics lies. We desire, by defending ourselves, in our community by every man putting a shotgun in his home, we desire non-antagonistic contradictions. We *must* defend ourselves. So when those cops come in the community to get down wrong, the *first* law is the law of survival. This is where it's at. We must organize We must respect the gun in a fashion that it's the man behind the gun who's dangerous. And there are thousands and thousands of cops in this country who are very, very dangerous for the black community.

So, let's come to the surface and think, come up to the surface of the whole situation. Black people in this country, war has been made upon them. Black people, don't sit down and say, oh, nothing's gonna happen, and hope nothing's gonna happen. Don't sit down and let a spontaneous riot happen in the streets where we get corralled and a lot of us are shot up, unorganized, when I say spontaneous; black people, organize! And black *leaders*, you got me up here! I'm only trying to contribute to the leadership. I was forced out here and it's necessary for me to do and I'm going to do my job. I'm saying that black leaders will get up and let the political power structure know where it's at and the changes we want and that if it doesn't happen, that *you* will have caused a political consequence in an organized fashion. The man doesn't have us outnumbered, he has us *out organized*! Come on, now, come up to the surface.

Now let's go back to our Brother Huey concerning his situation. Alright brothers and sisters, I want to say this here: Free Huey, Black Power, Black Power, and You are the Power, the Black Power, to free Huey. So, let's stand together, let's free Huey. I want to thank you.

Suggested Readings

Carter G. Woodson, *Negro Orators and Their Orations.* Washington, D.C., Associated Publishers, 1925. This is the most comprehensive volume on black speakers. However, it does not include speeches beyond the first quarter of this century. More recent speeches may be found in Charles Lomas, *The Agitator in American Society.* Englewood, New Jersey, 1968; Robert L. Scott and Wayne Brockriede, *The Rhetoric of Black Power.* New York, Harper and Row, 1969; and Roy L. Hill, *The Rhetoric of Racial Revolt.* Denver, The Golden Bell Press, 1964.

Related works are Herbert Aptheker, *A Documentary History of the Negro in the United States.* New York, Citadel, 1951; Frederick Douglass, *The Life and Times of Frederick Douglass, Written by Himself.* Boston, DeWolfe and Co., 1895; Howard Bell, "Expressions of Negro Militancy in the North 1840–1860," *The Journal of Negro History*, XLV, January, 1960; and Harvey Wish, ed. *The Negro Since Emancipation.* Englewood, New Jersey, Prentice-Hall, 1964.

For information on the Black Panthers, see *The Black Panther*, published weekly from Ministry of Information, Box 2967, Custom House, San Francisco, California 94126.

Additional Readings

Baldwin, James. *Nobody Knows My Name*. New York, Dial Press, 1961.

Bardolph, Richard. *The Negro Vanguard*. New York, Rinehart and Company, 1959.

Bennett, Lerone, Jr. *Before the Mayflower: A History of the Negro in America*. Chicago, Johnson Publishing Company, 1966.

————. *Confrontation: Black and White*. Chicago, Johnson Publishing Company, 1965.

Brink, William J. and Harris, Louis. *Black and White*. New York, Simon and Schuster, 1967.

Broom, Leonard and Glenn, Norval. *Transformation of the Negro American*. New York, Harper and Row, 1965.

Brotz, Howard, ed. *Negro Social and Political Thought 1850–1920*. New York, Basic Books, 1957.

Carmichael, Stokely and Hamilton, Charles. *Black Power: The Politics of Liberation in America*. New York, Vintage Books, 1964.

Chapman, Abraham, ed. *Black Voices*. New York, New American Library, 1968.

Clayton, Edward T. *The Negro Politician: His Success and Failure*. Chicago, Johnson Publishing Company, 1964.

Cruse, Harold. *The Crisis of the Negro Intellectual*. New York, William Morrow and Company, 1967

Daniel, Bradford. *Black, White and Grey.* New York, Sheed and Ward, 1964.

Ellison, Ralph. *The Invisible Man.* New York, Random House, 1952.

Embree, Edwin R. *13 Against the Odds.* New York, Viking Press, 1945.

Fager, Charles E. *White Reflections on Black Power.* Grand Rapids, William Eerdmans, 1967.

Fanon, Frantz. *Black Skin, White Masks.* New York, Grove Press, 1967.

————. *The Wretched of the Earth.* New York, Grove Press, 1968.

Gregory, Dick. *Nigger: An Autobiography.* New York, Dutton, 1964.

Hernton, Calvin C. *Sex and Racism in America.* Garden City, New York, Doubleday, 1965.

Isaacs, Harold R. *The New World of Negro Americans.* New York, The John Day Company, 1963.

Jacobs, Paul and Landau, Saul. *The New Radicals.* New York, Random House, 1966.

Jones, LeRoi. *The System of Dante's Hell.* New York, Grove Press, 1965.

Katz, William Loren. *Eyewitness: The Negro in American History.* New York, Pitman Publishing, 1967.

Killian, Lewis and Grigg, Charles. *Racial Crisis in America: Leadership in Crisis.* Englewood, New Jersey, Prentice-Hall, 1964.

King, Martin Luther, Jr. *Why We Can't Wait.* New York, Harper and Row, 1964.

Lincoln, C. Eric. *Black Muslims in America.* Boston, Beacon Press, 1961.

Logan, Rayford, ed. *What the Negro Wants.* Chapel Hill, North Carolina, University of North Carolina Press, 1944.

Loggins, Vernon. *The Negro Author: His Development in America.* New York, Columbia Press, 1931.

Marx, Gary T. *Protest and Prejudice: A Study of Belief in the Black Community.* New York, Harper and Row, 1967.

Meier, August and Rudwick, Elliot M. *From Plantation to Ghetto.* New York, Hill and Wang, 1966.

Murphy, Raymond and Elinson, Howard. *Problems and Prospects of the Negro Movement.* Belmont, California, Wadsworth Publishing, 1966.

Parsons, Talcott and Clark, Kenneth B. *The Negro American.* Boston, Houghton Mifflin, 1966.

Quarles, Benjamin. *The Negro in the Making of America.* New York, Collier Books, 1964.

Reddick, L. D. *Crusader Without Violence.* New York, Harper and Row, 1959.

Rose, Arnold M., ed. *Assuring Freedom to the Free.* Detroit, Wayne State University Press, 1964.

Rudwick, Elliott. *W. E. B. Du Bois: A Study in Minority Group Leadership.* Philadelphia, University of Pennsylvania Press, 1966.

Scott, Robert L. and Brockriede, Wayne. *The Rhetoric of Black Power,* New York, Harper and Row, 1969.

Thompson, Daniel C. *The Negro Leadership Class.* Englewood, New Jersey, Prentice-Hall, 1963.

Warren, Robert Penn. *Who Speaks for The Negro?* New York, Random House, 1965.

Waskow, Arthur I. *From Race-Riot to Sit-in 1919–1960.* Garden City, Doubleday, 1966.

Williams, John A. *The Man Who Cried I Am.* Boston, Little, Brown and Company, 1967.

Williams, Robert F. *Negroes With Guns.* New York, Marzani and Munsell, 1962.

Wish, Harvey. *The Negro Since Emancipation.* Englewood, New Jersey, Prentice-Hall, 1964.

Woodward, C. Vann. *The Strange Career of Jim Crow.* New York, Oxford University Press, 1955.

Index